THE FIVES COURT

Dedicated to Alice Rose Heal,
who would have loved the house and garden.

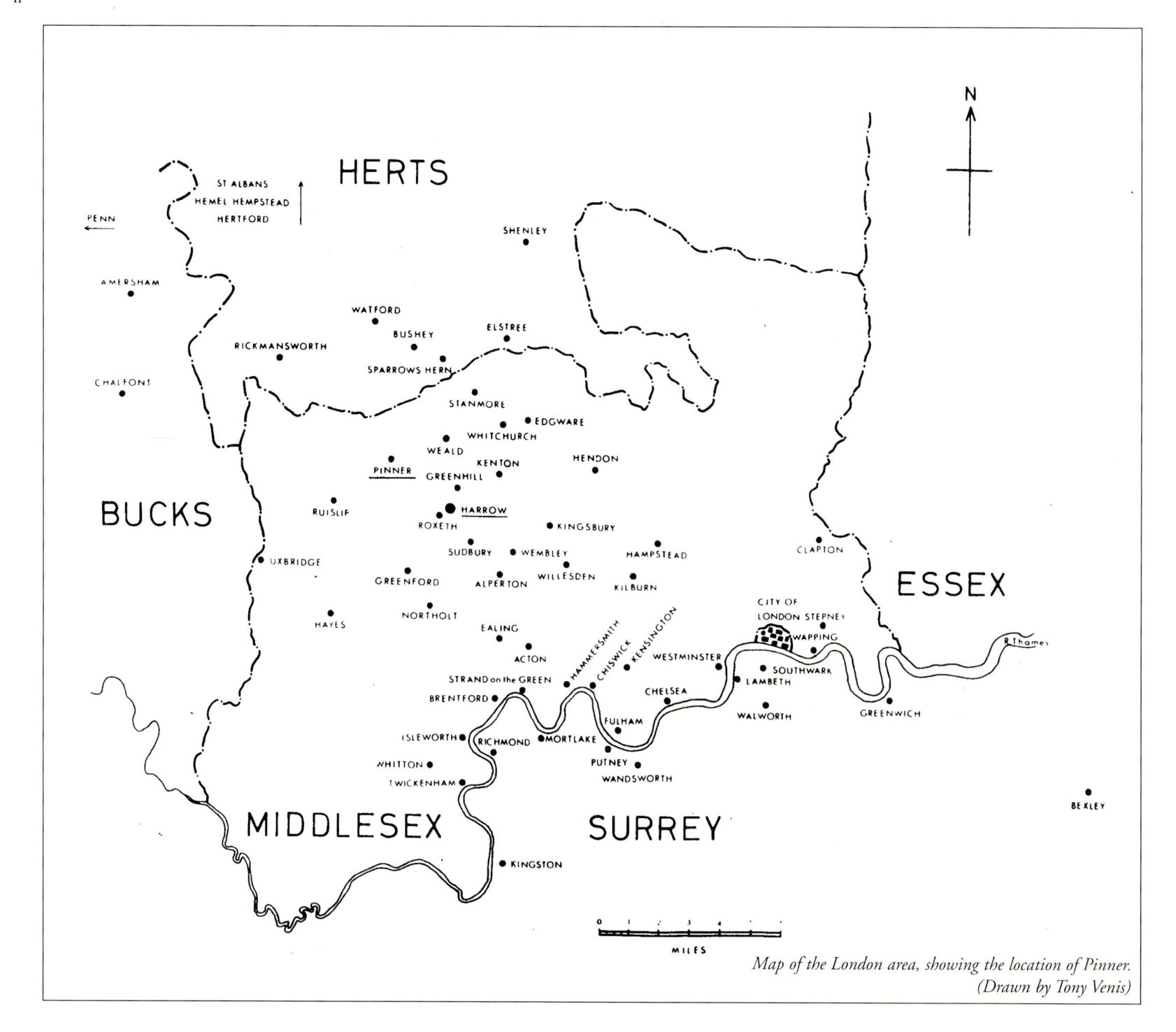

Map of the London area, showing the location of Pinner.
(Drawn by Tony Venis)

THE FIVES COURT

A CENTENARY

Jim Golland
with
Joanne Verden

The history of a house
in Moss Lane, Pinner, Middlesex,
its Architect, Cecil Brewer, FRIBA,
and the Heal Family for whom it was built.

Published by Joanne and Martin Verden, 2000.

Other books by Jim Golland:

> *The Harrow Apprentices*
> *The Guide Book to Harrow School*
> *When I was a Child*
> *The Illustrated History of Harrow School*
> *Heraldry at Harrow School*
> *Latin Inscriptions at Harrow School*
> *Not Winston, Just William?*
> *Fair Enough?*
> *Pinner to Paradise*

First Published in Great Britain, 2000.

All rights reserved. No part of this book may be reprinted or reproduced or utilised in any form by any electronic, mechanical or other means, now known or hereafter invented, including photocopying or recording or in any retrieval system, without permission in writing from the publishers.

Origination: Jim Golland, who has asserted the moral right to be identified as the author of this work in accordance with the Copyright, Designs and Patents Act, 1988.

Arrangement and design: Joanne Verden.

Printed by PMT Print Uxbridge 01895 233600.

Published by Joanne and Martin Verden, The Fives Court, Moss Lane, Pinner, Middlesex HA5 3AG.

ISBN: 0-9539131-0-4

Copyright ©Jim Golland, M.A., 2000.

Front cover picture:
A water colour impression of the east front of The Fives Court by Cecil Brewer, FRIBA.

Back cover picture:
West elevation of The Fives Court today by Ptolemy Dean, FRIBA

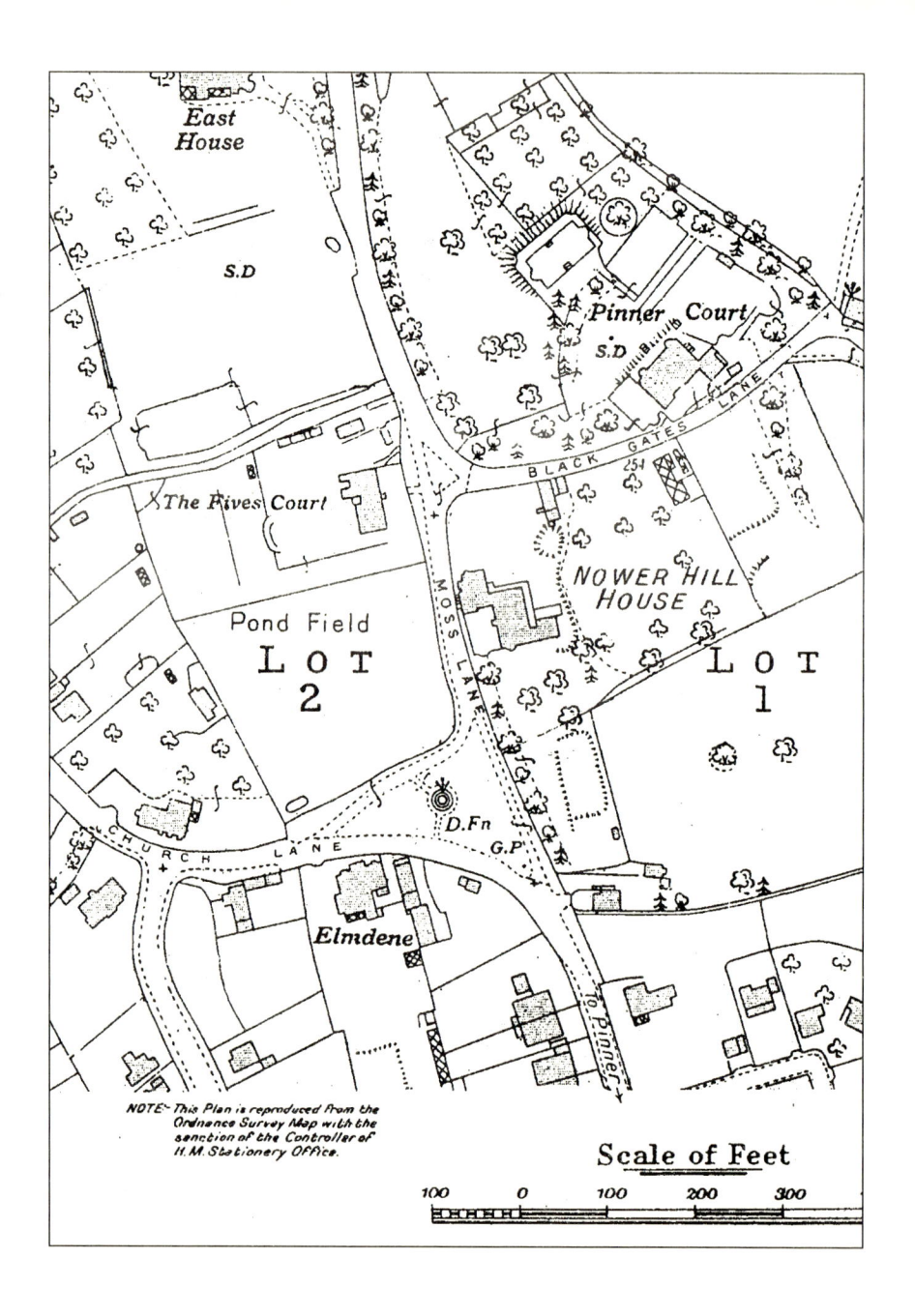

Moss Lane in 1939 showing Pinner Court, Nower Hill House and The Fives Court, with Wakeham's Hill (then called Blackgates Lane).

Contents

Preface:	Margaret Richardson, Curator of the Sir John Soane's Museum	ix
Foreword:	Oliver Heal	ix
Introduction:	Martin Verden	ix

The Fives Court:
    Its Location, Conception, Realisation and Extension   1

The House as a Home:
    Joanne Verden shows us round   5
    The earlier Heal Family and Nower Hill House   8
    Sir Ambrose Heal and his Family   12

The House as a Design. Architects with a Vision:
    Cecil Brewer   21
    Arnold Dunbar Smith   32

Fashions in Design:
    The Arts and Crafts Movement   33
    Design and Industries Association   37

Later Residents of The Fives Court   39

Appendix I	Heal and Brewer Family Trees	40
Appendix II	Life of Sir Ambrose Heal	41
Appendix III	His furniture designs	42
Appendix IV	Comments on his furniture	43
Appendix V	Books by Sir Ambrose Heal	44
Bibliography		44
Acknowledgements		45
Index		46

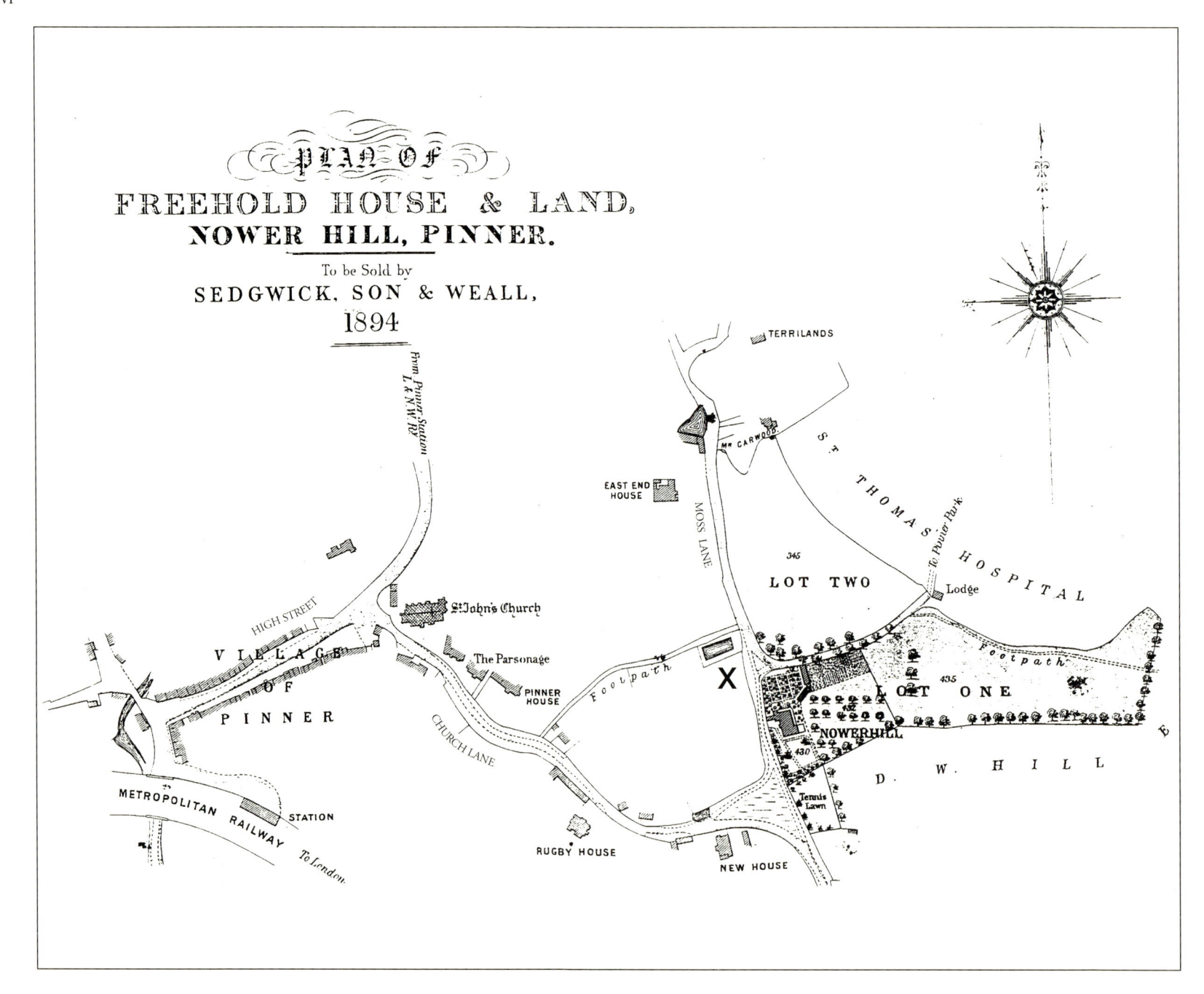

Pinner, in the sales brochure for 1894, when Nower Hill House was bought by Ambrose Heal, senior. It shows the site of The Fives Court (marked X) and its proximity to Pinner Station, the High Street, Pinner Church and Church Lane.

Illustrations

Map showing the location of Pinner	ii
Map of Moss Lane in 1939	iv
Map of Pinner in 1894	vi
The Fives Court: north elevation	viii
West elevation of The Fives Court: Ptolemy Dean	Frontispiece
Original plans for the house	1
Wakehams Hill, with Heal and Toovey families	2
A game of Fives in progress	2
Ambrose Heal leaning over the gate	3
The house seen from the east before 1908	3
Brewer's design for the hall	3
The Fives Court today from the east	4
Two reception rooms in Edwardian days	4
Bell pull	5
The west elevation	6
The loggia	6
The rose arbour	6
The music room	6
Suffragette notepaper	7
A garden party at Pinnercote	7
Nower Hill House design	8
John Harris Heal and Fanny Heal	9
Engraved billhead	9
Heal's salvage poster	9
Poster advertising Nower Hill for sale	10
The earlier house at Nower Hill	11
Handbill for a garden party at Nower Hill	11
Sir Ambrose Heal, FSA	12
Memorial tablet for Alice Rose Heal	13
Cecil Heal as a boy in the garden	14
Edith Heal at The Fives Court, expecting her first child	14
Pinner High Street	15
Cecil Heal in the wild flower meadow	15
Poster advertising Heal's	16
Trade Cards from the book by Ambrose Heal	17
A table and an advertisement designed by Ambrose Heal	18
Anthony Heal as a boy at The Fives Court	19
Anthony Heal	19
Heal monogram on drainpipe at Baylin's Farm	19
Impression of The Fives Court by Brewer	20
Cecil Brewer FRIBA	21
Passmore Edwards Settlement (Mary Ward House):	
South elevation	22
Main entrance	22
Residents' entrance	23
Nower Hill House: octagonal hall	23
The Fives Court being built	24
The Fives Court from the gardens of Nower Hill	24
Detail of a house at Westcott	25
Brewer's plan for the hall at The Fives Court	25
The National Museum of Wales at Cardiff	26
An earlier version of Heal's store in Tottenham Court Road	27
A letter from Brewer to the RIBA about his travels	27
Brewer's design for Heal's	28
Details from the frontage of Heal's	29
Plan for the gardens at The Fives Court	31
Spiral staircase at Heal's	31
Knocker from Nower Hill Cottage in The Chase	31
Sundial at Baylin's Farm	31
Arthur Dunbar Smith, FRIBA	32
William Morris	33
Hatch End Station	34
House by Charles Voysey at Sandgate, Kent	35
Harrow Heritage Trust plaque on The Cocoa Tree	35
Chair by Voysey	35
Grate by Smith and Brewer	37
Celtic knot design from The Fives Court ceiling	37
Louis Davis drawing for a window in Pinner Parish Church	38
Joanne and Martin Verden	39
Family tree of Heal and Brewer families	40
Part of a bedroom suite by Ambrose Heal	43
Arms of the Heal family	44
The Fives Court and Nower Hill House	50

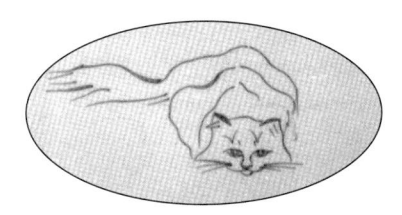

The north elevation of The Fives Court, showing the distinctive chimneys and the decorative kitchen window. (Photo: Gavin Stamp)

Preface by Margaret Richardson
Curator of the Sir John Soane's Museum

The architect Cecil Brewer is one of the unsung heroes of the Arts and Crafts Movement. With his partner A.Dunbar Smith, he won the competition in 1895 for the Mary Ward Settlement, which became one of the most original and influential buildings of the Movement. Sadly, Brewer died before the completion of two of their well-known schemes - the Museum of Wales in Cardiff and the Heal's building in Tottenham Court Road.

Consequently this delightful book is to be welcomed It describes in detail one of Brewer's best houses - The Fives Court, which has that primitive simplicity and tastefulness which Hermann Muthesius recognised as so characteristic of his work. But it also describes the relationship between Brewer and his cousin Ambrose Heal, the furniture designer and ideal client. Sharing the same interests in good craftsmanship and functional utility, they produced a perfect house which, in is evocation of the simplicity of an Arts and Crafts life, is so inspiring today.

Foreword by Oliver Heal

When I learnt that a book was to be produced to mark the centenary of the construction of The Fives Court, I thought it was a delightful idea. It is a home of great charm, which contains many distinctive features very typical of the style of the Arts & Crafts Movement, and I looked forward to knowing more about its design and history.

However, it came as a very pleasant surprise to find not only the history of the building but also a great deal of family history. Jim Golland is to be congratulated on all the information he has discovered about the Heal and Brewer families.

The Fives Court stands as a permanent memorial to the co-operation between two very gifted men, Cecil Brewer and Ambrose Heal, junior. Brewer, the architect, was only a year older than his cousin Heal, the shopkeeper, but Ambrose Heal in later life was to say that Cecil Brewer was his "closest friend, and to his inspiration in those early days, I owe everything in the way of design I may ever have done." It is very fitting that one hundred years later their co-operation should be commemorated with this book.

Oliver S. Heal
France

Introduction by the Owner

Joanne and I are indebted to Jim Golland, who has remarkably and patiently pieced together a fascinating tale of people and events associated with this house.

Creative visionaries save us from the banality of conformity through their contributions as philosophers, poets, composers, designers, painters, or architects. The Fives Court, designed by Cecil Brewer, cleverly manifests the ethos of the Arts and Crafts Movement.

New ideas for furniture expressed through the designs of the first occupant, Ambrose Heal, live on today in the showrooms of the Conrans and Habitats of this world.

It is a delight to recall that my father, Oscar Verden, who lived so close by in Pinnercote, Paines Lane, was also a business neighbour of Heal & Sons in Tottenham Court Road. He was a partner of Bartholomew & Fletcher, Furniture and Interior Designers. They furnished some of the public rooms for the transatlantic liner Queen Mary.

Women stand as equal in our society today, but Mrs Pankhurst had to fight a bitter battle to bring this about. The Fives Court played host to Pinner ladies who also had the strength and determination to press their case.

Any owner of this house can justly be proud of its history. English Heritage has listed the building, so that with foresight and care it will be preserved and we hope will continue to inspire those who live in it to make their dreams come true.

Martin Verden

*The west elevation of The Fives Court, seen from the garden,
by Ptolemy Dean, FRIBA, in 1999.*

THE FIVES COURT

The forces of fashion influence our lives even in the realm of architecture. Tastes alter and the style of one generation is anathema to the next. One person's dream house may not fulfil another family's needs. Yet sometimes a house so suits the requirements of its occupants that it continues to give pleasure over many years.

Pinner, in the London Borough of Harrow in north-west Middlesex, has such a house. It is one that celebrates its centenary with the Millennium, and one that marks an interesting period in the history of house design. It became a Grade II Listed house in December 1981 and was deeply admired by Sir John Betjeman. This book records something of its history and its significance, and tells the story of the family for whom it was built.

The house is The Fives Court in Moss Lane, designed by Cecil Brewer in 1900 for his cousin, Ambrose Heal, of the famous furnishing store in Tottenham Court Road. Brewer was a keen follower of the Arts and Crafts Movement, and just what that involved we shall see later.

What is it that makes this house so special?

Finding The House

You can reach this house quite easily from Pinner Station by walking up the High Street, bearing right at the church, passing Pinner House and turning down a narrow passage known as Blackgates. But perhaps the most fitting way in which to approach The Fives Court would be to take a train instead to Headstone Lane station and walk briskly across Pinner Park. The final climb up Nower Hill to the road known as Wakeham's Hill may leave you breathless, but glowing with the effort and the fresh air.

Like its original owner, and its architect, we will have shown our fondness for open air activity and exercise. A great walker, Ambrose Heal was also keen on tennis and that strange game beloved of public schools, known as fives, which is played not with a racket but with a gloved hand and a hard ball. He had played it at Marlborough College, and having to accommodate a court for it posed a particular problem for the architect.

Below you on the other side of Moss Lane is a building that at once seems different from other houses in the district. Perhaps it is the tall chimneys or the shape of the gate?

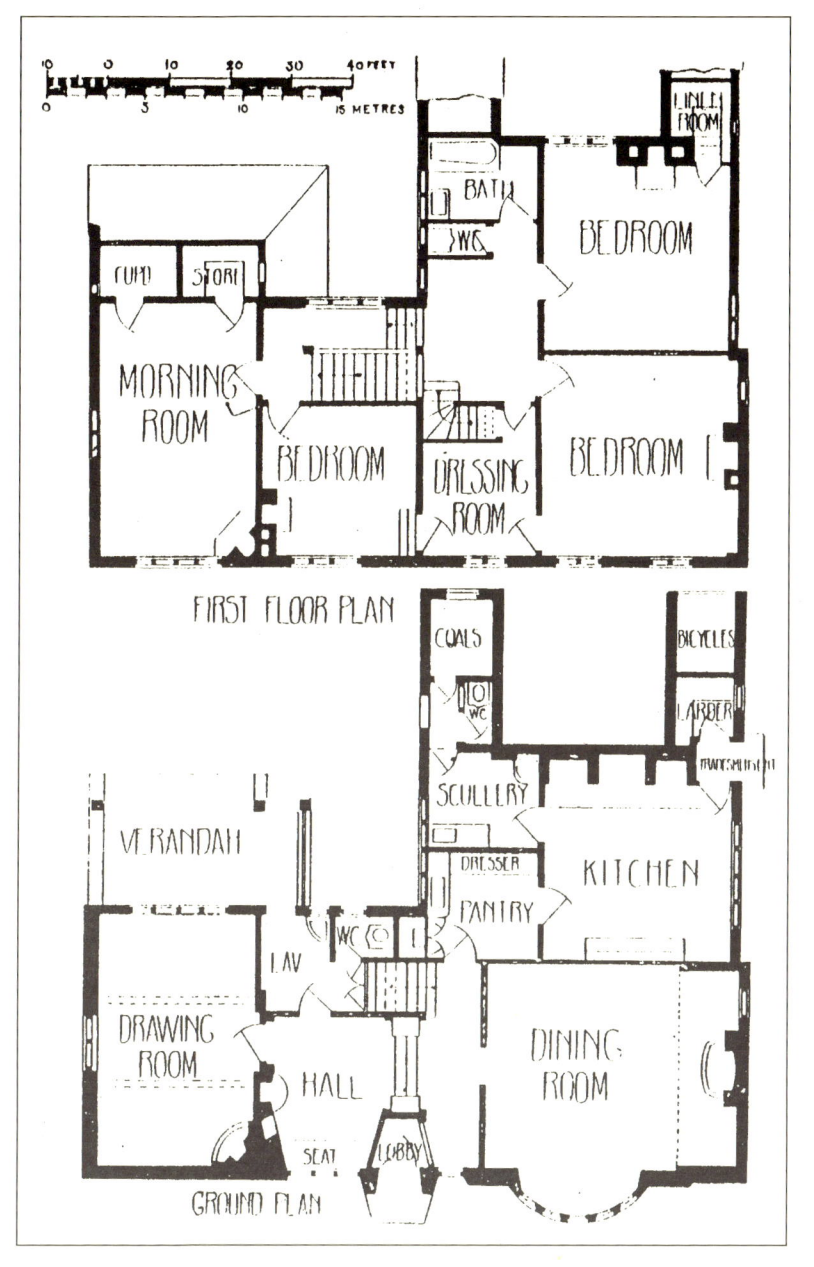

Brewer's original design for the house in 1900, with the top floor at the top of the page and the east front at the foot.
(RIBA Drawing Collection.)

The Conception

When Brewer started on his designs for The Fives Court, he was faced with several problems: a sloping site, a pond, and an owner who as well as being a close relation had definite ideas of his own. The architects of the day tended to listen to the ideas of their patrons, and Ambrose Heal was a designer himself and knew clearly what he wanted. Paramount was a fives court, and Brewer solved that difficulty with consummate ease, incorporating cycle sheds and fuel stores in the projecting wings.

Cecil Brewer and his partner Arthur Dunbar Smith were heavily influenced by members of the Arts and Crafts Movement, like Charles Voysey, whose own house, The Orchard at Chorley Wood, was praised by Pevsner for its long horizontal bands of windows and bold bare walls. *(See page 34)*

In designing The Fives Court, Brewer used a simpler version of Voysey's style, with more attention to natural colourings and texture, as well as the effects of light and shade. He was, like William Morris, concerned that his designs should reflect the function of the building: his chief criterion was fitness for purpose. He aimed to recreate the simplicity of a mediaeval cottage: "the tasteful application of the vernacular," as one critic described his work. Peter Davey described it as "a rough-cast, deep-rooted version of Voysey, without his pronounced horizontality."

The Realisation

The contemporary architect Ptolemy Dean has pointed out the many deliberate and delightfully characteristic touches in this house, such as Brewer's love of the octagon and of unusual angles, seen both in plan and in vertical decoration. *(See page 25)*

Lawrence Weaver, still writing in typical Victorian style only ten years after the house was built said, "It needs no soaring ambition to dwell in such a habitation. But it needs something which is almost as rare, an educated taste that sees wherein lies the essence of quiet beauty and informed mode of living, and infuses that essence into the substance of the dwelling and the spirit of domestic habits."

Wakeham's Hill, showing the triangle of land that still exists, and members of the Heal and Toovey families. (See page 19)

A game of fives in progress in the court on the west side of the house.

Its first owner, in his manner of furnishing and style of living, satisfied the intentions of the architects in their original concept, using not only contemporary pieces of furniture but items from the seventeenth and eighteenth centuries as well.

The Extension

In 1908, to accommodate a growing family, The Fives Court was extended, the music room being doubled in length to the south, with rooms for use as a day nursery above. The addition of extra rooms subsequent to the main building was a feature also of other houses designed by Smith and Brewer such as Nower Hill House, which until 1964 stood on the other side of Moss Lane.

Cleaning our muddy boots on the original scraper by the door, we pause to admire the interesting porch and the pattern of the tiles on the path. We pull the same bell that guests have used for a hundred years, and await our hosts.

The door opens and a warm welcome from the present owners invites you across the threshold. At once you are surprised by the cosiness of the small entrance lobby.

Ambrose Heal as a young man leaning over the gate.

The house and garden seen from Wakeham's Hill in a sketch by Cecil Brewer before the 1908 extension.

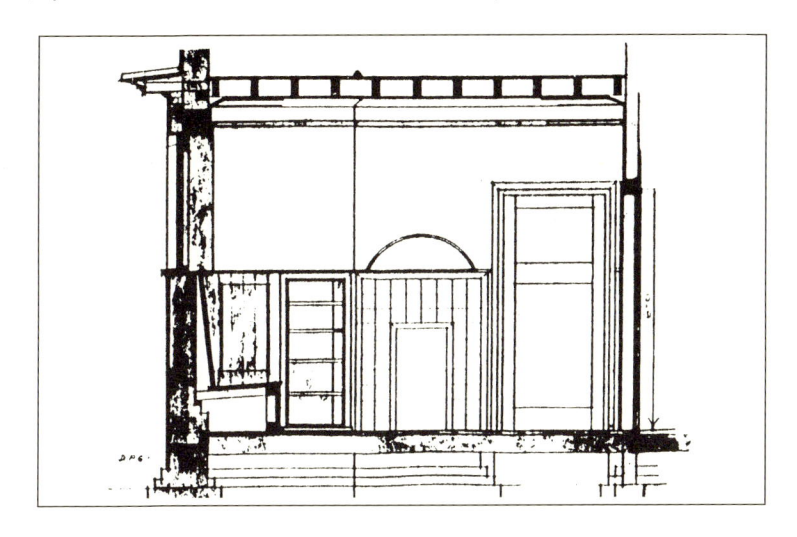

Brewer's design for the hall at The Fives Court, showing the bookcase, fireplace and elliptical moulding (RIBA Drawings Collection.)

4

The Fives Court today.
(Photo: Peter Saunders)

Sketches by Thomas Raffles Davison (1858-1937)
of the two reception rooms at The Fives Court in Edwardian days.

THE HOUSE AS A HOME
By Joanne Verden

Before you enter, glance up at the wide over-hanging roofline that provides shelter from the weather: the eaves are supported on metal brackets that form a regular pattern along the walls, echoing the rhythm of the window frames. Notice the window shutters on the front of the house, which faces east. We are woken by the early morning sun, but the shutters can be closed to filter bright sunlight, and so avoid damage to fabrics and furniture.

In the gable above is an octagonal window, hinged horizontally to allow for easier cleaning, and actually containing two windows, one within the other. The octagonal pattern is repeated in the tiles by the front door, which is still painted in its original green. The shape of the flattened arch on the wall above the door is repeated in the semi-circular Yorkstone doorstep.

Much of the charm of the house lies in these thoughtful and artistic details. Visitors first find themselves in a lobby, which serves to shelter the house from the elements. The hall does not set out to be palatial, but to have a fireplace, a bookcase, a window seat and three levels of ceiling height within a comparatively small space is an achievement. In the white wood panelling can be recognised the same design motif as in the oak front gate.

During the Second World War, the hall provided the security of an air-raid shelter, and was a self-contained place for the family to sleep. Through an archway, the staircase is hidden from view, allowing younger members of the family, if they wish, to escape upstairs unseen by adult visitors.

For family gatherings, there are two reception rooms. The larger one has two fireplaces, the original one in a corner, decorated with Arts and Crafts tiles, the other one in classic marble, inserted in the extension in 1908 and perhaps influenced in design by Sir John Soane. We call this the Music Room, as with a grand piano it is suitable for musical soirées. The teak floor with ebony marquetry is superb for dancing.

The smaller drawing room has great adaptability. Although it was originally the dining room, we find it too attractive for just that purpose. The oak fireplace area with a lowered ceiling is a cosy nook for a quiet read. However, the rest of the room has a higher ceiling with Celtic knot plaster work* as a frieze and a corona of wild roses forming a circle within a square. It may be no coincidence that Heal's first wife was named Alice Rose.

Pinner had an active suffragette group, and this room was probably where the Pinner branch of the Women's Social and Political Union held their meetings before and during the First World War, when Mrs Edith Heal was the Speakers' Secretary, Mrs Mark Verden the Treasurer and Miss Phyllis Verden the Literature Secretary.

Their Secretary, Mrs Terrero of Rockstone House, Paines Lane, was imprisoned in 1912 for breaking shop windows in Regent Street. Meetings were held at Pinnercote in Paines Lane, the home of Mr. & Mrs Mark Verden, my husband's grandparents. At other times they met at The Fives Court, possibly while in another room, Ambrose Heal and Cecil Brewer were planning the foundation of the Design and Industries Association. *(See page 37)* Subsequently, committees from the Pinner Local History Society, the Pinner Association and the Harrow Heritage Trust have met here to discuss local and Borough affairs.

That the Fives Court was built as a family house is evident from the "Perambulatory", designed for the baby's bassinet. The loggia beyond it faces west, an open-sided room exposed to the fresh air but sheltered by the eaves, its solid oak beams at one with the ethos of a country cottage. It gives the opportunity for eating or even sleeping outdoors, and, facing the westering sun it is a pleasant place to sit and enjoy an evening drink.

For large gatherings, the doors of the ground floor rooms can be thrown open to reveal a view from one end of the house to the other: at Christmas time, lights on the tree can sparkle all the way from north to south ends. White wood panelling is a decorative link between all three rooms.

Jacqueline Howe concluded after much research that the plasterwork was by G.P.Bankart (1866-1929), a member of the Bromsgrove Guild. (See page 36) He specialised in heavy foliated plasterwork as well as designing lead cisterns and rainwater heads. He exhibited at the Paris Exposition in 1900, along with Smith & Brewer. Mrs.Howe also thought it likely that the electrical fittings were by W.A.S. Benson, also of the Bromsgrove Guild.

West elevation of the house, showing the external fives court and the chimneys, capped with York stone as protection from the tall elm trees.

The rose arches (now the site of Amberley Close). Nower Hill House can be seen in the background.

(All these 1910 photos of the The Fives Court are by courtesy of Country Life Picture Library)

The loggia, used for outdoor eating and sleeping. Thick strong oak beams support the roof.

The music room with marble fireplace. A ventilation grille under the grate helps with the draught.

> **VOTES FOR WOMEN**
> The Women's Social and Political Union, Pinner
>
> COMMITTEE:
>
> Hon. Secretary:　　　Hon. Treasurer: Mrs. VERDEN　　　Speakers Secretary:
> Mrs. TERRERO　　　Literature Secretary: Miss VERDEN　　　Mrs. AMBROSE HEAL, jun.
> Rockstone House, Pinner　　　Votes Secretary: Miss BESSIE BARRETT　　　The Fives Court, Pinner
> (Headquarters for Local Union)　　　　　　Telephone No. 111 Pinner

Notepaper heading for Pinner's early Suffragettes.

On the first floor, the rooms for the Heal children were given as much thought as those for the adults. The night nursery had a corner fireplace with hand-painted cats on the surround, and large cupboards with rear windows, a most unusual feature but welcome when storing toys on dark days.

The day nursery had window seats with views over Tooke's Green and up Wakehams Hill. William Heath Robinson, the famous illustrator and eccentric cartoonist, lived along Moss Lane with his wife and young children. Perhaps the two families joined together for a stroll along the tree-lined lane.

An interesting feature is the care shown to provide a pleasant environment in the servants' quarters. The kitchen has an arched window of Palladian style, overlooking a secret garden, and the housekeeper's room on the second floor has as fine a fireplace as have the guest bedrooms.

The original area for the fives court was adapted in the 1950s to house the central heating boiler. I wonder how many balls had been through windows when the court was in use?

The whole garden has been steadily developed over the years. Crowds of scillas, daffodils, and fritillaries arrive in spring as they have done for decades.

Some time ago, when the late Anthony Heal came to show his son Oliver the house where he was born, he gave us some some old photos of the gardens of both Nower Hill House and The Fives Court. Some of these illustrate this book, and were used to recreate designs for wooden archways and trellis work in the garden.

A wisteria planted in 1909 is still scrambling up the south wall, where an inconspicuous trap door opens to facilitate clearing the ashes from the music room fireplace.

Pinner is still a good place in which to live, and it is satisfying to find a home here that offers advantages and common sense ideas from a hundred years ago.

A garden party at Pinnercote, Paines Lane, to support the Suffragette Movement.

*An impression of Nower Hill House, Pinner,
drawn by Cecil Brewer and including the plans. (See page 10)*

THE HEAL FAMILY

Sir Ambrose Heal, for whom The Fives Court was built, was a major force in the commercial life of London and a furniture designer of high quality. But, like his parents, he was also an antiquarian with a passion for collecting and a deep interest in his own family history.

It is thanks to him that we can now trace the family back to its early days in 16th century Somerset (and possibly even to Heals alive in the 13th century).

Anyone interested in the details may contact the author of this book; briefly, Ambrose Heal, a farmer of Kingston Deverill, near Gillingham, Dorset, married Rachel Harris in 1771. When he died in 1812 he did not mention his two sons, John Harris Heal and Ambrose, in his will: supposition is that they had quarrelled and that the boys left home to set up in business in London.

John Harris Heal started as a dresser of the then fashionable ostrich feathers with a firm on the site of the Empire Theatre in Leicester Square. He married Fanny Brewer, and when his employer went bankrupt, he set up in business for himself in premises near Oxford Street. In 1818 he moved to a farmhouse near 203 Tottenham Court Road, where he established a company making feather beds and mattresses.

On his death in 1833, his widow continued the business, moving to its present site at 196 Tottenham Court Road in 1840 in what had been livery stables for country gentlemen visiting London. She stayed until her son, **John Harris Heal junior**, was old enough to take over in 1845. Under him, the firm prospered, making eiderdown quilts, luxurious French mattresses with East India wool and horsehair, and goose-feather beds. The name "became synonymous with the best that money could buy." They advertised on railway platforms and in all 77 of the novels of Charles Dickens.

By the time of the Great Exhibition of 1851, in which J.H.Heal took part, he was making bedroom furniture in dark woods suitable for Gothic houses, as well as expensive iron and brass bedsteads that were proof against bed bugs. He designed portable furniture for army officers to take with them on campaigns.

A new store for Heal's was built in 1854, to the designs of J. Morant Lockyer in a florid Italian Renaissance style. It was then one of the largest in London. Two years later John Harris Heal moved his home from Woburn Lodge, near the shop, to an

John Harris Heal, junior (1811-76)

Fanny Heal, his mother and the widow of the Founder.

Two of the earlier generation, Ambrose Heal's father and grandmother.

Engraved billhead for Fanny Heal & Son, 1840.

Poster advertising feathers for sale by Heal's after a fire at their warehouse, 1871.

PINNER.

Within Ten Minutes' walk of Pinner Station on the Metropolitan Railway, and One and a Half Miles of the Station on the London and North-Western Railway, and Close to the Church and Village.

PARTICULARS AND CONDITIONS OF SALE

OF THE VERY DESIRABLE

FREEHOLD PROPERTY

KNOWN AS

"NOWER HILL,"

Comprising an OLD-FASHIONED

FAMILY RESIDENCE,

WITH

EXCELLENT GARDENS,

PRODUCTIVE ORCHARD AND PASTURE LAND

In the rear, the whole embracing an area of about

SIX ACRES;

ALSO AN

ENCLOSURE OF PASTURE LAND,

CONTAINING ABOUT

FOUR ACRES,

Having EXTENSIVE FRONTAGES TO TWO ROADS, offering

Excellent Sites for the Erection of Good Residences,

Which are in great demand in this favourite locality.

The whole of the Property is Freehold and exempt from Land Tax and Tithe Rent Charge.

POSSESSION WILL BE GIVEN ON COMPLETION OF THE PURCHASE.

WHICH WILL BE SOLD BY AUCTION, BY

SEDGWICK, SON & WEALL,

AT THE AUCTION MART, TOKENHOUSE YARD, LONDON, E.C.

On WEDNESDAY, MAY the 9th, 1894, at 2 o'clock,
By direction of the Owner.

May be viewed only by orders from the Auctioneers. Particulars, Plans, and Conditions of Sale may be had at the Mart, Tokenhouse Yard, E.C.; at the usual Hotels in the neighbourhood; of MESSRS. HYDE, TANDY, MAHON & SAYER, Solicitors, 33, Ely Place, Holborn, London, E.C., and of MESSRS. SEDGWICK, SON & WEALL, Land and Timber Surveyors, Estate Agents and Auctioneers, 88, High Street, Watford, Herts.   [PEACOCK, PRINTER, WATFORD

Poster advertising Nower Hill House for sale in 1894.

isolated farm of 113 acres in Finchley, called Grass Farm. His property portfolio continued to expand, and he bought up plots all over London. The firm built a cabinet-making factory in their old timber yard behind the shop.

He introduced the idea of fitting up small rooms in his store to show off the bedroom furniture: though now the normal practice, this was an innovation in 1866.

In 1834, at South Stoke, Somerset, he had married his cousin, Ann Standerwick Heal, daughter of the Ambrose who had come to London with the founder and had started a similar business himself. They had eleven children.

John Harris Heal died in 1876 and control of the firm passed, not to his sons (his eldest, though a partner, did not head the firm until 1894) but to his son-in-law and cousin, **Alfred Brewer**, father of the architect of The Fives Court.

Of the eleven children, Harris Heal took over the firm on Alfred Brewer's retirement in 1894; John was a leather merchant of Finchley; Frank was a barrister and lived at Frith Manor, Mill Hill; and Ambrose became Chairman of Heal's in 1906 when his brother Harris died.

Ambrose Heal, senior, was born in 1847 in St. Pancras, and remained devoted to that district. He had lived at Amedée Villa, Crouch End, until the attractions of Pinner drew him to what was becoming a very fashionable place to live. In 1895, he bought an old farmhouse on Nower Hill from the Graham family, but lived at The Grange in Church Lane until the house had been renovated.

The firm of Smith and Brewer was asked to extend and modify the building, installing a billiard room and other amenities. The work was done by a local builder, James Darvel, who could well have been employed also on The Fives Court.

In his sketch for the proposed alterations Brewer said that Nower Hill House as it stood was of no definite character. "Various excresseurs had been built on between 1830 and 1870. The house presents a mixture of work in brick, plaster and half timber." He said that the roof was half tiles, half slates.

(For Heal and Brewer family trees, see Appendix I.)

In the eighteen years that Ambrose Heal lived in Pinner he became one of its most prominent residents and interested himself particularly in helping the Pinner Men's Club and the Horticultural Society. He was a keen church-goer and a sidesman at the parish church of St.John's at the top of Pinner High Street. An antiquarian, he entertained the members of the London and Middlesex Archaeological Society on their visit to Pinner.

Pinner in his day was undergoing the beginning of its transformation from a rural village to a modern suburb. In 1897, Heal was patron of the Headstone Races, though his own horse that year came in last. There were still only 3000 people in the village. Members of the Royal Academy, like Buxton Knight, regularly came to paint the picturesque rural High Street, complete with cattle and sheep. Kate Greenaway and her friend Helen Allingham, the artists, visited Waxwell Lane and East End and left us memorable views of the cottages there.

At the turn of the century, though, as villagers celebrated the Relief of Mafeking in the Boer War or the Coronation of Edward VII, Moss Lane "idyllic in its secluded beauty" according to the Vicar, had already been invaded by what he called a "regiment of perky little red villas." A chance to turn fields at Barrow Point into a recreation ground was lost when developers bought them instead. The pleasant routines of garden parties, horticultural shows and village sports would soon be lost for ever in the welter of the World War.

When Ambrose Heal died in 1913 whilst on holiday in Scotland, he left his magnificent array of topographical material* to St.Pancras Library.

His wife, formerly Emily Maria Stephenson, was also a collector, and continued to take a keen interest in Pinner. She always intended that her archive material of obituaries, photographs and press cuttings about the village and its personalities should form the basis of a Pinner Local Studies Centre. In fact, these archives, known as the Heal Collection, are now housed in the Harrow Reference Library. Mrs Heal died in 1938, and is buried with her husband in Paines Lane Cemetery.

The shop in Tottenham Court Road continued to expand and between 1894 and 1912 their trade had quadrupled under Ambrose's careful management.

He was succeeded by his son, **Ambrose Heal, junior**, (later Sir Ambrose, the first occupant of The Fives Court).

*This vast collection of pictures and press cuttings is now on microfilm and can be seen at Holborn Library.

A Christmas card from Ambrose Heal, showing Nower Hill House, known locally as Cabbage Hall, as it was before conversion.

Handbill for a garden party at Nower Hill in 1916.

PINNER WAR WORKERS' GUILD.

A

GARDEN PARTY

In Aid of the Funds of the above,

WILL BE HELD AT

NOWER HILL,

(kindly lent by Mrs. Heal),

— ON —

Saturday, July 8th, 1916,

3 till 7.30 p.m.

SIR AMBROSE HEAL

Sir Ambrose Heal, F.S.A. (1872-1959)

Ambrose Heal was born at Crouch End in 1872, and after preparatory schools, went to Marlborough in 1885, leaving after a leg injury in a house football match in 1887 ("and so escaped being superannuated," he wrote). He recuperated whilst staying with a tutor in Westgate, Kent, where he was joined by his cousin, Cecil Brewer, who had been similarly injured at Clifton College. Following further study at the Slade School, in 1890 Ambrose was apprenticed to a cabinet-maker in Warwick for two years. After six months with Graham & Biddle of Oxford Street, he joined the family business in 1893, working in the bedding factory and becoming a partner in 1898.

At Torquay in 1895 he had married Alice Rose Rippingille, a lady some twelve years his senior. She was the daughter of Alexander, a patentee of oil stoves, from Birmingham. They went to live near his parents at Firgrove*, 4 Nower Hill, Pinner.

Their son Cecil was born in that house in 1896, and was possibly named after Ambrose's architect cousin, Cecil Brewer. The latter was asked to design a new house for them on a plot of land bought by Ambrose senior opposite his own house. In March 1901 they moved into The Fives Court, Moss Lane, Pinner.

Alice Rose was already ill with cancer and had little time to enjoy her new house. She died shortly afterwards, on May 4th 1901, aged only 41. She was buried in a grave in the cemetery, commemorated by an unusual copper memorial in Arts and Crafts style, incorporating the rose motif used in the ceiling of the drawing room at The Fives Court.

Three years later Ambrose was married again, to Edith Todhunter, a doctor's daughter who studied art, Greek myths, costume design and heraldry. With this knowledge, she was able to help Ambrose with his publications.

Ambrose Heal junior had a freckled skin, with fluffy gold-red hair, small eyes behind spectacles with round 18th-century frames perched on a pointed nose, and a thin mouth; he was of medium height, small footed with a light tread; he had a high, breathy, faintly superior voice, rather affected in tone as if he was looking down his nose through half-closed eyes.

He was deemed a remarkable man, blessed with super-human energy and many talents. He was devoted to fives, squash, tennis and walking. Described as an artist-craftsman with a business-like air and method, one of his greatest commercial skills was his ability to grasp and respond to a challenge without necessarily believing in it.

As well as being a businessman, he was a keen historian and writer, and an antiquarian like his father, as his *Times* obituary in 1959 testifies:

"He studied his predecessors, the cabinet-makers and upholsterers of London from 1660 onwards. Their trade cards fascinated him, and in 1925 he had already collected sufficient to publish a substantial volume. As time passed, the collection grew enormously and in 1953 he published what must surely be the definitive work on the subject, beautifully indexed and illustrated. His passion for craftsmanship also found expression in his great work on the London goldsmiths, in which he was able to add no fewer than 3,600 names to the 2,800 already known.

---

*A semi-detached five-bedroomed villa, later to become a school, it was owned by Mr Dunbar Thomas of Elmdene, who built most of the Edwardian houses in Moss Lane.

"Calligraphy, again a craft, also greatly interested him, and his book (to which Stanley Morison contributed a preface on the development of handwriting) is a notable contribution to the study of the little-known subject.

"Last but not least may be mentioned his volume on the signboards of old London shops, in 1948."

The width of his interests can be seen from the books he wrote. In *London Tradesmen's Cards of the XVIII Century*, he said: "The old tradesman's card is a straightforward announcement of his wares.... It does this without palaver, without unseemly parade, and without pretence that it is either a sermon or a novelette.... It avoids those errors against good taste into which some of our modern advertisers are so easily beguiled. The lettering in the early examples is almost uniformly of a high standard of achievement; the design, or as advertising men say, the 'layout', is dignified and well-spaced, the ornament well drawn and the copper-plate engraving is highly accomplished.

"To anyone with a liking for old things the Trade Card must make an irresistible appeal. It is so convincingly of its own time. There is no affectation of the pseudo-antique, nor does it attempt to be cleverly up to date. It has the quaintness of its period, the characteristic phrasing, the picturesque quality of the old-world wares, described by fine resonant names: Grograms, Padusoys, Callimancoes, Lutestrings, Prunellas* and the like, long since fallen into disuse, but everyday words of their time."

He also appreciates the "quality of a romance and the excitement of a bargain sale" when seeing some of the prices for old materials shown on the cards. Collecting Trade Cards, he found, gave him pleasure because so few did so, and he saw it, not as an investment or a way to impress friends, but as an opportunity for studying heraldry, architecture and costume (with the help here of his wife) as well as revealing artistic techniques.

Here we can see his love of colourful antiquities and something of his interest in typography and advertising, which came to the fore in his development of the public image of Heal's between the wars.

Others of his kin, he suggested, collect horse brasses, insurance plates, or valentines. He himself collected old books.

*All names of silk materials

The memorial to Alice Rose Heal in Paines Lane Cemetery, showing a similar rose motif to the one in the drawing room at The Fives Court.

Cecil Heal as a boy in the gardens of The Fives Court in the early years of the century.

Edith Heal at The Fives Court, expecting their first child.

In a passage that should appeal to all local historians, he wrote:

"The path of the collector of Trade Cards lies alongside that of the diligent seeker after the lesser known antiquities. He is the man who patiently puts together print by print, cutting by cutting, the history of some small lovable village now engulfed in Greater Suburbdom."

One biographer said of him, "He was a man of vision and extraordinary energy; a sensitive designer, with an adventurous imagination; an inspired shopkeeper who pioneered modern design, from typography to architecture. He was self-assured, with unfailing energy, perpetually on the crest of a wave."

Part of his energies were spent on keeping happy not only his wives but a number of mistresses, including Mrs (later Lady) Prudence Maufe, with whom he dined nearly every day.* She was the wife of the architect who later remodelled the shop front for the firm and designed Guildford Cathedral. A classically beautiful Edwardian lady, wearing leg of mutton sleeves, long skirts and buckle shoes, she was in charge of the Mansard Gallery on the fourth floor of Heal's. Her embroidered kneelers can still be seen at Guildford, and when she died in 1976 she left behind a collection of over 2000 silver shoe buckles. Remarkably, she also designed railway carriages for the GWR.

She remarked that Ambrose "was generally disliked and feared, as he had the eye of an eagle. His dominant personality and complete integrity inspired his staff with admiration and respect: he was a benign dictator." He spent the week in town, which gave him freedom to see his mistresses, none of whom ever prevented him from being devoted to his wife, to whom he returned home at the weekends.

Another close friend was the playwright and novelist, Dodie Smith, whom he met when he gave her a job in the Mansard Gallery in his store. He designed a new bed-sitting room for her flat in Fitzroy Square, in cream and gold with white walls with no pictures, a custom-built ebonised desk, a black metal-topped dining table, a speckled black and white carpet, black Bluthner piano, black glass flower vases, silver candlesticks, and black and silver cushions and curtains.

He frequently admired Dodie's clothes and allowed her to wear an orange shawl from Heal's, remarking rather acidly, "If she wants to dress up as a Polish peasant I see no reason to stop her." He would not, however, let her open a dress department.

---

*Valerie Grove, Dear Dodie, page 60

He received from Dodie an elaborate Valentine that he kept for over 30 years until he was in his late 80s.

A founder member of the Everyman Theatre in Hampstead, Ambrose took an interest in Dodie Smith's plays; he liked the script of *Autumn Crocus* (1930) so much that he sent it to his friend Sir Nigel Playfair, and rang her from Beaconsfield one Sunday to say that Playfair was prepared to take it up. When told that Basil Dean had already made an offer, he said, "The silly fellow should have offered earlier." He never had the slightest doubt about its success, and after seeing the play with friends he allowed her to work only part-time for Heal's, giving her more opportunity for playwriting.

Dodie sent him the script of *I Capture the Castle* and he revelled in it, giving her a detailed criticism: he couldn't appreciate the farcical bear hunt scene but liked the music, religion and the Vicar with his Madeira, so pleasant and wise. "I enjoyed it like good sherry and crumbly biscuits, crumbs and all." He adored her (self-) portrait as Topaz. Dodie in turn read his *Signboards* with a magnifying glass, whilst listening to the strains of Handel. He sent her a bouquet of lilies for the first night of *Bonnet Over the Windmill* (1937), and she sent him sugared almonds from America, which made him call her his "Sugar Plum Fairy". Later, she became famous as the writer of the lovable *One Hundred and One Dalmatians*.

Dodie did not find him as amusing a companion as Alec Beesley, later her husband. Ambrose was unable to see the fun in Thurber, whom her husband much admired. After Dodie married in 1939 he wrote, belatedly, in February 1940, "Tell Beazley ("He always referred to Alec in this superior mis-spelled way," she complained) I always felt he was cast for a big part & have no doubt he is set for a long run to good houses." Towards the end of his life, his letters to her became increasingly affectionate and even skittish, riddled with innuendoes.

His mistresses thought him mean, saying that he only paid for what he had to, but he did pay for holidays and presents of jewellery, watches, clothes, an emerald ring, a fine table, and a typewriter for them. When Dodie Smith asked for a rise, he looked disagreeable and said it was utterly out of the question. He asked her why she needed one, and what were her expenses. When he thought Dodie made out a good case, he raised her salary after all.

He disliked anything being sold for less than it cost, whatever its current worth, and himself sold a broken toy at full price as the customer would assume it had been broken in transit.

Pinner High Street before the First World War with the Heals' pony and trap, and the family dog.

Cecil Heal in the wild flower meadow to the west of the house, which can be seen in the background before its extension in 1908.

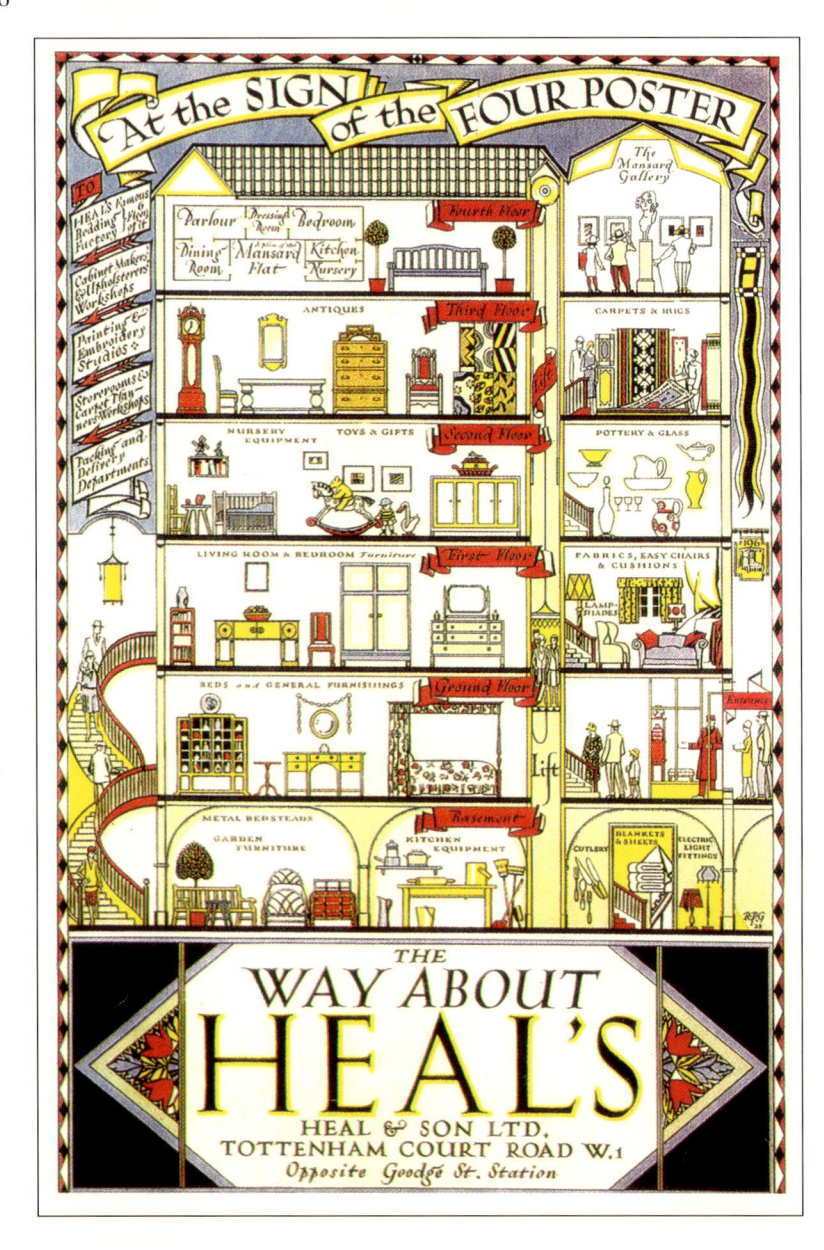

Poster advertising Heal's, showing some of the many delights available in the shop.

However, his main concern was the welfare of Heal's and the design of furniture. He started with simple oak pieces suitable for weekend cottages in the country, such as some he made for F.W. Troup at Letchworth in 1905. Ambrose Heal was knighted in 1933 for improving design standards, and had moved on to more sophisticated products in steel and aluminium by 1935. He always acknowledged his debt to Cecil Brewer's genius for design. *(See page 29)* The latter's passion for octagons, for instance, was echoed in a mirror of that shape Ambrose used on his own dressing table at Beaconsfield.

As we see in a further extract from his obituary, **"He was perhaps one of the great artists and craftsmen of his time. His introduction of strong but simple and beautiful lines to the modern world of furniture did probably as much of importance and significance as did the great masters of the 18th century. He was not unlike them, also, in his love of working with the rarer and more exquisite woods. Yet in spite of this contribution which he made towards the new orientation in the world of cabinet-making, he had a respect which almost amounted to veneration for the beautiful productions of Britain, France, and Spain before ugliness overtook us, and he was as happy to deal in such work as he was to see people admiring and buying his own pieces, which were the products of his fine perception and understanding.**

"His early training at the bench gave him a sound feeling for the relationship between craftsmanship and design, and keen appreciation for the possibilities as well as the limitations of woods and other raw materials. The beauty of wood was a passion and like a true craftsman, he was capable of designing a piece of furniture, the main artistic merit of which was its display of particularly finely marked timber.

"His period in control of the family business saw an immense widening in scope as well as reputation. He added departments for the sale of almost all household requirements, and displayed a notable gift in selecting the right men to control these new enterprises.

"Earliest and most important was the department of antique furniture. Pottery was added later and made a notable contribution to the fame of the business, as also did the textile and carpet departments. More modest were the departments for kitchen and bathroom requirements but even in these his fine catholic taste was observable.

Three of the elaborate Trade Cards from Ambrose's book. They were intended as advertisements, but showed some of the aspects of heraldry, costume or calligraphy that appealed to him.

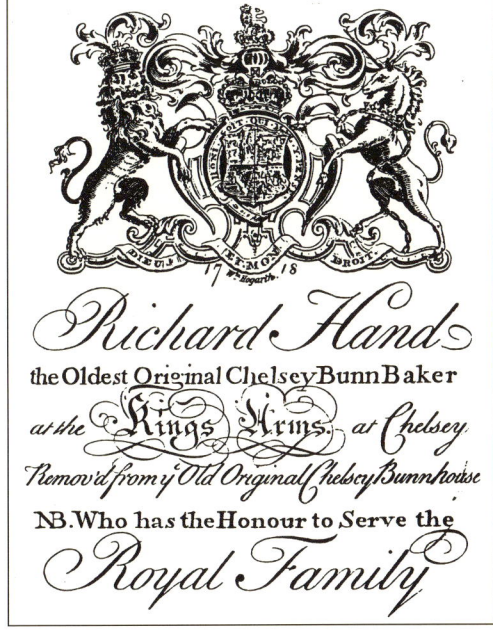

The card advertising the Chelsey Bunn Baker was attributed to William Hogarth.

"In 1929 a great gallery was made in the top floor of the building, which was the scene of many notable exhibitions of pictures and furniture." *¹

"Heal's," said Julia Goodden, "avoided a wholesale rush into the uglier fruits of mechanisation by cherishing and promoting the excellence of craftsmanship in its own cabinet-making factory and by having the good fortune to have Ambrose Heal - a man of vision and extraordinary energy - in the family." *²

Ambrose and Edith moved to Little Bekkons, Station Road, Beaconsfield, in March 1917, sub-letting The Fives Court to tenants. Two years later, they moved to Baylin's Farm, Knotty Green, just outside Beaconsfield, an Elizabethan farmhouse that was extended in 1925 by Edward Maufe and by the firm of Forbes & Tate. It still contains many mementoes of Ambrose, with the family cypher on a sundial, in the brickwork of the extension, on drain heads, and on a rain water tank originally from The Fives Court.

Lady Edith died there in 1946, and the playwright Dodie Smith wrote to Ambrose with a tribute to her unassuming manner: she had introduced their children to Dodie as though they were being presented to royalty. She had a graceful brand of good manners and a low, very beautiful speaking voice. Her husband spoke of Edith's "simple considerate ways, the fine gallant spirit behind that quiet modest demeanour."

Sir Ambrose died on November 15th, 1959, aged 87. He is buried beside the memorial to his second wife in Penn Churchyard, where there is also a striking memorial cross designed by Maufe.

For the Heal and Brewer Family Trees, see Appendix I.
A summary of the main events of Ambrose Heal's life is given in Appendix II.
Examples of his furniture design are listed in Appendix III.
A representative selection of comments about his furniture-making, giving some idea of his range can be seen in Appendix IV.
For a list of his books see Appendix V.

---

*¹ ©*Times*, 17.11.1959
*² Goodden page 17

A table designed by Ambrose Heal.
(Photo JG, by kind permission of the Geffrye Museum)

A typical advertisement for Heal's, featuring the four-poster bed first introduced as an emblem by Ambrose Heal in 1904, here used for the firm's centenary in 1910.

CHILDREN

Cecil, Ambrose's son by his first wife, followed his father to Marlborough, where he played cricket for the 1st XI. In 1915, when still only eighteen years old, he joined the Army and was killed by a sniper in Belgium.

Ambrose's first daughter, Barbara, by his second wife, died at one year old in 1906. In the loggia at The Fives Court are the figures of two angels. Do they, perhaps, commemorate these sad events in the early years of the house?

A second daughter, Pamela, was born in 1908 at The Fives Court and died in Dublin in 1983.

His son Anthony Standerwick Heal was born at The Fives Court in 1907. As a boy, he was clearly inspired by his father, who had set aside a room on the top floor of the house as a carpentry room for him. After an apprenticeship with the designer Gordon Russell in Gloucestershire, he joined Heal's in 1929, becoming Managing Director in 1936 and Chairman from 1952 to 1981. He was Master of the Furniture Makers' Guild in 1959. Passionately fond of motor racing, he was a founder member of the Vintage Sports Car Club, and in his spare time raced vintage cars and displayed steam engines at rallies. His wife, Theodora, (1906-1992) was a sculptress. He died at Penn, Bucks, in 1995. One son, Ambrose, still lives at Baylin's Farm, and the other, Oliver, in France.

Ambrose's second son, John Christopher, was born at The Fives Court in 1911 and ran the Drawing Office at Heal's after studying architecture at Sidney Sussex College, Cambridge. Remembered for his great sense of fun, he designed many items of furniture for the store and was appointed Design Director in 1961. He died in 1985.

As well as Sir Ambrose, Ambrose Heal senior had four other children, one of whom, known affectionately as Daisy, married the son of Dr Dove of Church Lane, Pinner, in 1905. In the same year her brother Ralph married the daughter of Arthur Toovey, a solicitor who also lived in Church Lane. Ralph had been educated at Marlborough and Malvern and rose to become Managing Director of Heal's.

One of the Heal children, probably Anthony, lending a helping hand in the meadow. The house had now been extended. The picture seems typical of those idyllic days just before the First World War.

Anthony Heal (1907-1995)

Rain-water head in Baylin's Farm, with the initials of Ambrose and Edith Heal and rose emblems.

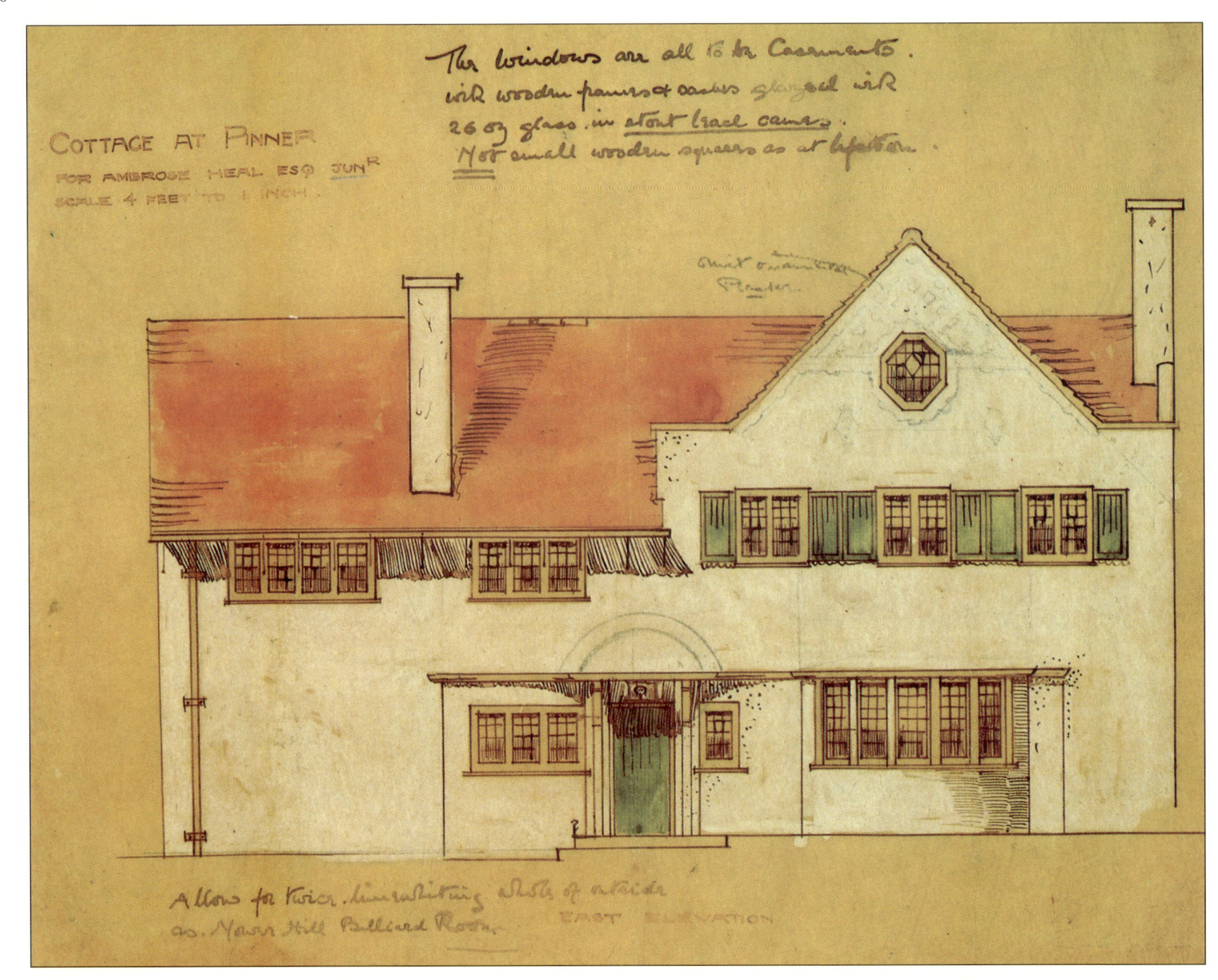

*Brewer's water-colour design for The Fives Court, with his inserted
comments, calling, for instance, for the omission of the ornamental plaster.*

THE HOUSE AS A DESIGN:
The Architect: CECIL BREWER, F.R.I.B.A.
(1871-1918)

Cecil Claude Brewer was born at 6 Endsleigh Street, Tavistock Square, in December 1871, and baptised at St. Pancras Old Church in August, 1873.

He was the youngest son of Alfred and Ann Brewer. Alfred was a partner in Heal & Son. Mrs Brewer was formerly Ann Heal,[*1] the sister of Ambrose Heal senior of Nower Hill House in Pinner, so Cecil was a cousin of Ambrose Heal junior.

Extremely youthful and slight in appearance, Cecil exuded self-confidence. "There was always something of the boy about him, not only in look and voice but in his zest for adventure," said a friend. He is said to have spoken in a childish treble and on one occasion to have appeared at a committee meeting dressed as a toddler.

With a short, compact body but very long legs, he was naturally lithe and agile, delighting in such bodily exercises as riding, dancing and cycling. He had organising ability, tact and powers of persuasion, as well as being an accomplished debater.

From 1886 to 1888, Cecil Brewer attended Clifton College, and then trained as an architect in London, winning a gold medal from the Royal Academy Schools. As a pupil of Frank Baggallay, the President, he worked for three years at the Architectural Association, being awarded their silver medal. A travelling scholarship enabled him to visit Brittany, and in 1894 he won the Pugin Prize for the drawings he made there.

Two years later, a Pugin Studentship from the Royal Institute of British Architects enabled him to travel extensively. After looking at churches in Essex and in great detail at Hedingham Castle, he toured France, Italy, the Netherlands, and Belgium, studying museums, libraries and picture galleries.[*2]

[*1] *Ann was also the daughter of John Harris Heal, whose mother was born Fanny Brewer, Alfred's great-aunt. (See page 9 and the Family Trees on page 40)*
[*2] *Later he was to become deeply interested in German and other European designers, and just before the outbreak of war in 1914 visited an exhibition in Cologne with Ambrose Heal junior, from which he returned full of enthusiasm for all things German. "I am now an apostle of much German work," he wrote. During the War, however, he modified his opinion: "The Germans have not got nearly as far I think towards providing good country houses as we have, or the best of the Americans. There is a very self-conscious striving after the new, whereas the conditions are not new and all that is wanted are reasonable houses for reasonable folk."*

Cecil Brewer

He set up in practice as an architect and he was only 24 in 1895, when he and his partner, Arnold Dunbar Smith, won a competition for the design of the **Passmore Edwards Settlement** in Tavistock Place, Bloomsbury. This was a community building and hostel and deserves a book or at least a chapter to itself. It changed its name to the Mary Ward Settlement after the death in 1921 of Mrs Humphry Ward, the novelist and grand-daughter of Thomas Arnold of Rugby. It was the writing of her novel, *Robert Elsmere*, about a young priest who found his faith by helping the poor, that had inspired her to found the settlement.

She was greatly concerned at the conditions of the poorer inhabitants of London, and founded a hostel for young professionals, University Hall, modelled on the success of Toynbee Hall in the East End. Smith and Brewer stayed there among other young men, who were intended by Mrs Ward to help bridge the gap between rich and poor and bring some culture to the masses by living amongst them and giving lectures and concerts and mounting exhibitions.

Their centre for this work was too distant from the hostel and Mrs Ward enrolled the support of a newspaper baron living near her in Bloomsbury, John Passmore Edwards. With his large donations she was able to commission a new building on the lands of the Duke of Bedford. The new hostel combined living quarters with a concert hall, lecture rooms, a gymnasium and craft workshops. It was soon attracting two thousand visitors a week to activities that included lectures by people like Sidney Webb and Seebohm Rowntree.

It still stands in Tavistock Place, south of Euston and St. Pancras stations, its green shutters immediately reminiscent of The Fives Court. The initials of the Passmore Edwards Settlement are on the rain water heads. Interesting railings catch the eye, along with symbolic decorations of trees and eggs, indicative of life and social rebirth. A massive entrance porch derived from Rudolf Steiner leads to a humble wooden door, the whole intended to give dignity to the building but put locals at their ease.

Inside, an octagonal lobby, heart shaped motifs on the furniture and individually designed fire grates all demonstrate the designers' individuality. They combine the public world of the concert hall and gymnasium with the private apartments in subtle ways. It is certainly a strange amalgam of styles, with Norman Shaw windows on the top floor, overhanging eaves of the kind used by Charles Voysey, interesting stepped windows on the staircases, and chimneys hidden from the road. A side entrance for residents is shaped like a funnel. Beaten copper panels indicate the two entrances to the hall. From the start, the building was lit by electricity and centrally heated. Clearly the young architects were aware of contemporary ideas.*

The German architectural authority, Hermann Muthesius, described the design as combining "extreme tastefulness with a primitive simplicity that bordered on the vernacular." Writing in the *RIBA Journal* in 1935, H.M.Fletcher described this work as "brilliant but immature". Dennis Farr called the plan "a gracefully balanced composition, intimate in scale, yet with a judicious formal symmetry." Pevsner thought it was one of the most charming pieces of architecture of its time in London. Margaret Richardson said it was one of the most original and influential buildings of the Arts and Crafts Movement. Mary Ward herself felt that the idealism of her social programme was reflected in the architecture.

Wendy Kaplan in her book on Charles Rennie Mackintosh goes so far as to say that elements of the latter's famous School of Art in Glasgow were inspired by Smith and Brewer's winning design. Their home for handicapped children next door at 9 Tavistock Place in 1903 was much less innovative, though still impressive in a Wren revival style.

---

*For fuller details, see Adrian Forty, in The Architects' Journal, *August 1989*.

The Mary Ward Settlement, 1895. The entrance porchway is flanked by separate doors for the audience and the artistes to enter the concert hall. The influence of Norman Shaw and Voysey can be seen in the roof line details.

The imposing main entrance surmounted by symbolic eggs, inspired by W.R. Lethaby. The actual doorway is small, and was designed to make local residents feel at home as they attended lectures.

The Residents' Entrance to the Mary Ward Settlement in Tavistock Place, London.

The octagonal hall in Nower Hill House. Round arches with a central keystone, as in the Mary Ward Setttlement, surmount the china cabinets, and flattened arches lead to other rooms.

Among the unsuccessful contestants for the design competition was Edward Prior, whose Music School at Harrow still adorns the Hill like a galleon breasting the waves. The judge who awarded the prize to Smith & Brewer was Norman Shaw, designer in 1891 of New Scotland Yard and, some twenty years earlier, of Grimsdyke, later to become the home of W.S.Gilbert at Harrow Weald.

With this background, Smith and Brewer started out on a busy practice of house and building design, their first major commission being in 1899 for a Sanatorium at Nayland, near Sudbury in Suffolk, which accommodated forty tubercular patients and was a landmark in hospital construction.

With such strong family connections, it is not surprising that Ambrose Heal senior asked Cecil Brewer to refurbish **Nower Hill House** in Pinner when he moved there in 1895 and to carry out alterations for some years after that. On a sloping 10-acre site, Brewer converted a mediaeval farmhouse, known locally as Cabbage Hall, into a substantial residence, complete with a hooded doorway over a copper studded entrance door, and an octagonal hall.

The house had several unusual features. The entrance to the dining room was down steps on either side of a recess containing a sideboard. There was an inner hall, as later at The Fives Court, and an unusual complex of living rooms, library, and billiards room that could form a circulatory area for social occasions.

Like many of his contemporaries, Brewer regarded the garden as an extension of the house, and carefully laid out a rose bed, an orchard, and lawns for tennis and croquet together with an interesting sundial, which, decorated with a Heal monogram, is now at Baylin's Farm, Beaconsfield.

When Ambrose's son married in 1895, he came to Pinner and rented a house near his father in Nower Hill whilst he was looking for a house of his own. Early in 1900 Ambrose senior bought four acres of land for £1000 from C.A.Woodbridge. They comprised two fields across the road from Nower Hill House, one abutting on Tooke's Green, the other and more northerly one adjoining Monks' Walk, now Blackgates, a passage that leads from Church Lane to Moss Lane.

It was on this latter field that Brewer was asked to design a house for Ambrose, junior. It would incorporate a court for Ambrose's favourite game of fives, that he had played at school. Brewer worked on the plans for **The Fives Court** in the summer of 1900, and the house was first occupied in March 1901.

The Fives Court being built in 1901, using wooden scaffold poles.

The Fives Court seen from the luxuriant gardens of Nower Hill House. Notice the archway of elms over the gate and the double row of elms on the right.

The house was in fact owned by Ambrose senior and leased to the son. When it was valued for taxation purposes in 1914 it was described as a well built house with ten rooms and two bathrooms.

As well as The Fives Court, Brewer also designed a gardener's cottage for Ambrose Heal senior in 1901, which still stands in The Chase, Pinner, a fine example of artistic design applied to a more modest dwelling, with vaulted corridors, interesting door furniture and an unusual corner fireplace.

Other local buildings on which he worked included The Glade at Harrow Weald (later Whytewayes old people's home), and Capesthorne on the Uxbridge Road. Between 1906 and 1913 he planned alterations for Thomas Forbes at East House in Moss Lane (since demolished). When Mr Forbes left Pinner in 1919, Dunbar Smith designed a house for him called Rushymead at Coleshill, near Amersham.

Among their first successful forays into domestic architecture were a house in 1899 for the Humphry Wards at Little Barley End, near Tring in Hertfordshire, and the rebuilding a year later of Stocks Farm on the same estate.

The years from 1890 to the First World War in 1914 were a period of great activity in the building of country houses. Architects here were doing work that was eagerly studied abroad, raising our architectural credit to a peak that it has not often reached.

"In this good company the names of Smith and Brewer stand high, stand indeed with the highest," said H.M.Fletcher. "Their country houses, to be found mostly in the home counties and East Anglia, have an individual flavour, but it is never exaggerated into eccentricity; they are based on tradition but never archaistic; and there is always a touch of novelty in planning and detail, a reasonableness and elegance which save them from vulgar exuberance on the one side and from the equally bombastic and much more self-conscious quality known as starkness on the other.

"Their work has a gaiety, an enjoyment in what they are doing, which comes from mastery of planning, design and the use of materials. This mastery was largely due to their early training in the Arts and Crafts movement and their familiarity with its leaders, particularly Lethaby. What an impression of cleanness, athletic vitality and distinction!"

The Macmillan Dictionary of Art said that Smith and Brewer had a far greater architectural vocabulary than the majority of their contemporaries and that their works were of the highest quality of design and construction.

Perhaps they had read these words from a lecture to the Royal Academy Schools in 1885 by the great architect, G.F. Bodley: "Little and infrequent touches of beauty, grafted onto a well proportioned fabric will give a building a tender grace, and it will be a delight to all passers-by. Be not afraid of richness and beauty when you can get it."*

In 1906 they started their designs for several houses on a new estate at **Westcott**, near Dorking, still much in demand today. One, originally known as Springbank, has projecting eaves supported on metal brackets as at The Fives Court and is designed to fit into a corner site with great ingenuity. The Pinner house has an octagonal window that gives a touch of originality; the Westcott house has an octagonal hall and study above. Both houses have three storeys, with spacious accommodation for servants. Both deal attractively with the problems of a sloping site.

One unusual assignment tackled by them was the sympathetic conversion in 1907 of a Georgian town house just off Piccadilly in London for use as a new home for the **Albermarle Club.** Particularly remarkable are their beautifully curved main staircase and the graceful pair of smaller flights on the first floor. The club buildings combine delicacy of detail and exquisite plaster work with strength and clean lines.

The largest and finest of their designs for big country houses was at **Ditton Place,** near Cuckfield in Sussex. It contains many individual touches of style such as the marble surround to the fireplace, with its chequered border.

Elected a full member of the Art Workers' Guild in 1901, Brewer was on the committee by 1906, when he was elected a Fellow of the RIBA.

In 1911 he was awarded a Godwin Bursary to visit the USA and Canada, and produced a 150-page report on some fifty museums and art galleries in those countries for the RIBA. He found that many famous museums were decorative buildings but totally unsuited to their job of displaying artefacts. He claimed that the Albright Art Gallery in Buffalo, New York was "the most nearly perfect". The astonishing amount of travel and study on this visit severely affected his health.

*Anscombe page 25

Detail from a house at Westcott, showing the octagonal hall and study above.

Design for the lobby and hall in The Fives Court by Cecil Brewer, showing an interesting use of angles.
(RIBA Drawings Collection.)

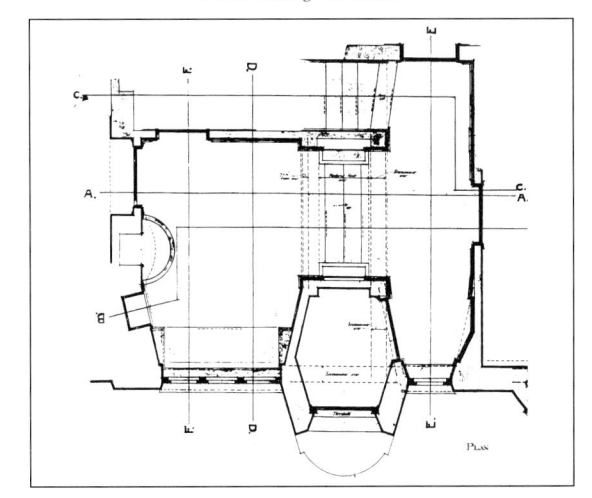

The National Museum of Wales at Cardiff. (Courtesy: RIBA)

Smith and Brewer's most well-known achievement was in winning another competition, this time to design the **National Museum of Wales** in Cardiff. Here they moved away from designing small vernacular houses to undertake a public building of classical proportions in a kind of American "Beaux-Arts" style. As such, it could bear comparison with the Paris Opera House and the Palais de Justice in Brussels.

In it, they solved brilliantly the problems of adjusting to existing grand neighbours, such as the City Hall and the University, whose architects had also entered the competition. On what was described as "the most magnificent civic site in the British Isles," their brief compelled them to create an exterior in harmony with the other buildings in Cathays Park, but the interiors reveal several personal touches. Smith's placing of the storage rooms on the outside of the viewing galleries is said to have been largely instrumental in their winning the prize. Their main dome overcame the problems that had fooled John Nash in his royal palace designs, and the building is lit by a number of smaller domes.

Started in 1910, but not opened until 1927, the Museum was designed as a national monument. But it is more than this. The architects paid particular attention to concentrating light on the exhibits and no architectural frills were allowed to distract the visitors' attention from these, resulting in a "simplicity bordering on severity." This made the museum a place of education for ordinary visitors rather than just a vast store room in which to keep national treasures.

This impressive building cost a quarter of a million pounds, and became a model for others to imitate, with its spacious entrance hall, interesting ventilation grilles, special provision for the reserve collections, grand staircases, and attention to lighting. Its fine sculpture court and inner garden were built over in 1993. The Museum's own Guide Book in 1937 declared that this was "one of the best designed buildings for its purpose in existence."

Its collection of Impressionist paintings is said to be the finest outside the Louvre, and its Natural History Galleries are vivid re-creations of the Welsh landscapes through the ages.

The illustration opposite shows some of the striking sculptures* decorating the exterior, representing the history of Wales and its Industries.

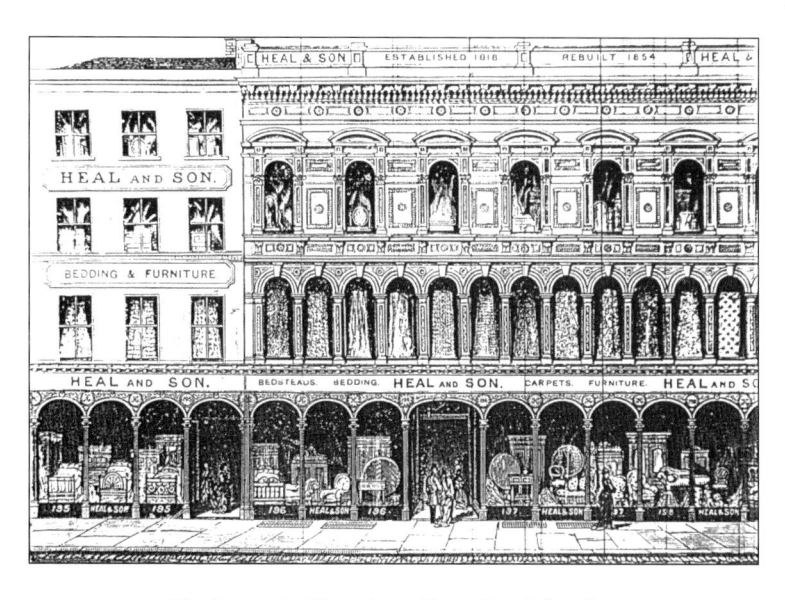

---

*By Richard Garbe, Gilbert Bayes, T.S. Clapperton, Bertram Pegram and David Evans.

Heal's store in Tottenham Court Road, London, as redesigned by J. Morant Lockyer in 1853.

An extract from a letter written in 1897 by Brewer to the Royal Institute of British Architects in connection with his award, in which he asks for his report on his visit to be returned to him for revision before publication.

Brewer's idealised view of his design for Heal's new shop front, 1916.

In 1912, Brewer had started to design a new frontage for **Heal's furniture shop** in Tottenham Court Road and a new bedding factory to the rear. Despite the wartime shortage of raw materials, building was completed in 1916. This was a landmark in the development of shop architecture, and is still greatly admired. Its steel frame has enormous floor to ceiling windows recessed behind a colonnade, and heraldic cast-iron plaques; inside is a stunning spiral staircase.

"Among the tatterdemalion buildings in that road the premises of Heal and Son hold the attention like a rhythmic ceremonial pageant," wrote H.M. Fletcher. "It is the most completely satisfying piece of modern shop architecture in London." "It is one of the best pieces of London street architecture in the present century," agreed *The Architect and Building News* in 1933. A judge later called it "a novel building of an artistic character." *The Macmillan Dictionary of Art* refers to the windows as being "set back to provide a strong shadow, thereby enhancing the effect of solidity and providing cover for viewers."

Before the Second World War, Heal's premises were refurbished and the frontage extended by the architect Edward Maufe, famous for Guildford Cathedral and the R.A.F. Memorial at Runnymede. He tried to remain faithful to Brewer's original designs and was so successful that Mr Meikle, then running the firm of Smith and Brewer, sued him for infringing Brewer's copyright. When Fitzroy Robinson extended the store even further in 1962, the unbroken facade still retained the rhythms of Brewer's design and contained what was said to be the longest continuous run of non-reflective plate glass windows in London.

Along with Ambrose Heal junior, Brewer was a founder member in May 1915 of the Design and Industries Association (DIA), and became its Secretary. The Association still exists, but its formation led to the creation of the Council for Industrial Design, now the Design Council. *(See page 37)* In addition to his secretarial work, he was also involved in planning for the reconstruction of the country after the war, and in February 1918 he prepared with the DIA a report for the Minister of Reconstruction, Dr (later Viscount) Addison, of Pretty Corner, Northwood and, latterly, of Brewer's own village of Radnage.

Its impressively ponderous title was *On the Encouragement of Small Industrial Centres to Assist in the Reconstruction of Rural Life and in the Employment of Discharged Soldiers, with a Preliminary Note upon the Relation of Handwork to Such Reconstruction.*

This suggested that small country towns could be invigorated after the War by the State establishing small factory units of from fifty to a hundred and fifty workers using local materials for such activities as making baskets, leather goods or ornamental ironwork.

Ambrose Heal had met his cousin at a seaside boarding house when both were recuperating after sporting accidents at school. In a speech in 1953, he declared,

"By this happy coincidence I came under his magnetic influence. For the next twenty years he was my closest friend and to his inspiration in those early days I owe everything in the way of design I may ever have done. He had a remarkable and lovable personality: had he lived he would have taken a very high place among the architects of his day. At his early death during the First War, he was already known by half a dozen pieces of brilliant work."

In his later years Brewer was hampered by illness, and for two years or more his friends feared for his life. "All the time I have known him he was delicate and subject to attacks of rheumatic fevers, pleurisy and then heart weakness," wrote his mentor, Lethaby.

These were perhaps made worse by an accident early in 1916, when a workman fell on him whilst he was inspecting the alterations to Heal's shop. He wrote to a friend in the DIA.: "I have come off second best in a combat between Design and Industry. Industry, in the person of an aged labourer at Heal's falling from a roof, espied Design in the person of your Secretary below him and alighted with both feet in the small of Design's back. They carried off the discomfited remains of Design in a Taxi Cab and he nurses in his bed a very sore back and a grievance against Industry."*

A month later he was taken ill with influenza and bronchitis, which in turn affected his already weak heart: "I am feeling stronger and fitter but Harley Street where I went yesterday looked and talked very gravely, and apparently a three-month complete rest is the least ill I have to fear. Bronchitis has apparently played the devil with the heart, which was always an inefficient organ & further trouble with bronchitis would be likely to leave the heart quite unfit for even the work I give it to do."

He had lived at 6 Queen Street, Bloomsbury, but his deteriorating health meant that rest in the countryside became

---
RIBA Manuscript Library.

Two views of Heal's shop in Tottenham Court Road, showing (Above), on the left, the Fitzroy Robinson extension in 1962, to the north of Brewer's 1916 reconstruction, seen on the right.

(Below): Brewer's building on the left, with Edward Maufe's southern extension on the right, with larger dormer windows. It was this faithful continuation of Brewer's design just before the last war that led to the 1941 court case for breach of copyright.

essential, and he went to live at Town End Farm, Radnage, six miles north of High Wycombe. "He recuperated so quickly and his spirits so soon rekindled that only his guarding wife* can have constantly realised how serious it all was," wrote Lethaby.

In spite of his increasing frailty, Brewer never gave in, displaying intense vitality to the last. "Not strong, he would not spare himself, often not leaving work until after midnight," said a colleague. "Nothing could be neglected nor be slurred over and finally the frail thread of life snapped."

He died of rheumatic fever and heart disease at Radnage on 10 August 1918 aged only 47, and was cremated at Golders Green on August 14th.

What is Brewer's claim to fame? Little has been written about him, but his untimely death while not yet fifty brought forth several expressions of regret at a promise unfulfilled. He had worn himself out by hard work. His business partner, Dunbar Smith, paid this tribute to him:

"It is certain that he had a genius for making friends and that his personality impressed even those who scarcely knew him, and the welcome that gleamed through his glasses was a thing that his friends could never forget. Very many will mourn him and feel that his death has removed one of the vital influences of present-day architecture.

"As an architect, his great natural gifts were enhanced by his extraordinary thoroughness and power of application. Early association with the Arts and Crafts Movement led him to acquire an intimate knowledge of all the trades and crafts connected with building, but his mind was of too architectural a bent to leave him content with craftsmanship as an end in itself.

"Latterly he saw architecture as a matter of fine planning, ordered massing and intellectual expression. Being an accomplished draughtsman and something more than accomplished water colourist, his plans were a delight; admirably practical, they were always shapely and fertile in new combinations. Ornament he used sparingly; his subtlety in design was such that he could afford a certain austerity of treatment, relying less upon richness of detail than upon the play of light and shade that results from delicate changes of plane. His sense of proportion was almost unerring, and the strength of his designs was tempered, not impaired, by their grace. The outstanding quality of Brewer's work was freshness."

"The double burden of work with his busy practice and with the Design and Industries Association hastened his death," said one obituary. "He faced the inevitable with great courage and fearlessness and simply went over peacefully and quietly. He is another bright, clever spirit that has left us before his energies flagged. In fact it was that restless energy of his that exhausted his remaining strength: in the end his mind could not rest and it wore his feeble body out."*

Let his other friends speak of him: "It is difficult to think of him as a leader, yet he led. He showed an unquenchable interest and a fresh youthfulness of soul, but his gallant spirit was bound to a body unequal to its burden. So infectious was his mental activity that a talk with Brewer was sovereign against depression and slackness; at the sight of such a spirit battling against difficulties you were shamed out of either.

"He was always lovable, because always generous. Reckless in tilting at institutions and even at persons that met his disapproval, he was enthusiastic for causes, eager and friendly and possessed of unsuspected powers of thinking, expression, and organisation. He radiated a rare human sympathy especially for those who were persecuted by convention or oppressed by officialdom."

Some of that reckless tilting can be seen in his letters and papers preserved in the RIBA Library. His caustic comments on contemporary design or on the more pedantic members of the DIA or of the Arts Workers' Guild show his wit and at times his irascibility:

"Heraldry could still be a fine living thing in the hands of a vigorous designer, far removed from the anaemic trash served up in stationery and silversmiths' departments. A fine set of regimental coats of arms could bring kudos to a store." (*A Lesson to Storekeepers*).

He had married Irene Macdonald at Haslemere, Surrey, in 1904. Her father George was a friend of Ruskin and Morris. He was a lay preacher and independent minister, as well as a novelist and poet, and wrote over thirty books, including mystical romances and children's stories. Readers may recall from their childhood his lines,

> Where did you come from, Baby dear?
> Out of the everywhere into here.
> Where did you get your eyes so blue?
> Out of the sky as I came through.

Her brother Greville was a consultant surgeon at King's College Hospital and her sister Winifred, Lady Troup, married a Permanent Under Secretary at the Home Office.

---

*Carrington.

Of various colleagues he wrote, "He is a most unbusinesslike dreamer." "I was driven wild by his fluffy English." "Their machine-made brains triumph." "We want bedrock men, not pushers and charlatans who never lose an opportunity."

Even his cousin, Ambrose Heal, did not escape. "My three years with him on the DIA have taught me to expect no ideas from him," he wrote to a friend. "His motto seems to be, 'Take all, give nothing.' I have a growing feeling that his influence is too great and that he himself values that influence a little too consciously."

Perhaps, though, the last word must rest with Brewer's obituary:

> "His powers had certainly not reached their full height at the time of his death and masterly as are the finest of his completed works, the loss to English architecture must be reckoned yet more by the greater things he would have done had he been spared to live his full term; if he had lived he certainly would have made even more important contributions to the new era of building (after the war)."

Pinner is proud to have two complete buildings designed by Cecil Brewer.

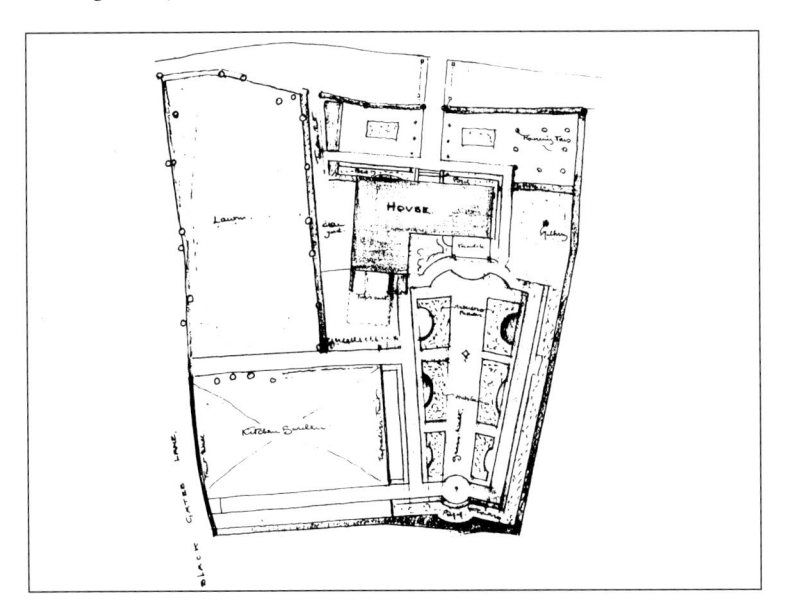

Plan for the garden at The Fives Court by Cecil Brewer.

The spiral staircase in Heal's shop. As in The Fives Court, climbing the stairs is made easier by the low risers.

The door knocker from Nower Hill Cottage, The Chase, Pinner, designed by Brewer.

The sundial from Nower Hill House now at Baylin's Farm, with the monogram for A. & E. Heal by Brewer.

The partner:
ARTHUR DUNBAR SMITH, F.R.I.B.A. (1866-1933)

Brewer's partner was five years his senior and survived him by fifteen years. He was born in Islington on December 2nd, 1866, and after a private school education, he attended Brighton School of Art. In 1883, he was articled to J.G.Gibbins of Brighton, who had worked in the studios of William Burges, designer of Harrow School Speech Room. Like Brewer, Smith received further training with the Architectural Association, with the Royal Academy in 1890, and with other architects in London like Walter Millard and Frank Baggallay.

He won a Godwin Bursary from the RIBA. A quiet, modest, retiring, indeed intensely shy man, his early years had not been easy. He seems to have overcome any personal suffering by hard work.

In 1895 aged 29 he went into partnership with the young Cecil Brewer. He hated public speaking, but his good humour made him a good friend. Their natures complemented each other but their aims were so harmonious "that the quality of their work would in no way suffer if either were left to do it single-handed." One of Brewer's assistants later said that Smith had the more highly-trained analytical faculties, but Brewer possessed "indescribable verve." Smith was a perfectionist, and did an immense amount of research for each of his projects. It was probable that he knew more about the design of museums and the lighting of art galleries than any other living architect. Brewer was thought to have more artistic talent, while Smith had the ability to make the best use of a confined space.

Mr Justice Uthwatt, giving judgement in the infringement of copyright case in 1941, said, "If indulgence in atmosphere was the natural bent of one, the other could be relied upon to see that his partner's ideas were translated into tactile effects."

Dunbar Smith's work can be admired at the "singularly complete and satisfying" Lecture Rooms in Mill Lane in Cambridge and in the Fitzwilliam Museum in that city. There, the galleries are divided into intimate "rooms" by projecting storage cupboards, thus avoiding the overpowering vistas of massed ranks of pictures seen in many galleries such as the Louvre in Paris. Once again, Smith paid great attention to lighting and some would consider the Fitzwilliam to have the best-lit galleries in Europe.

It was he who completed the additions to the Sheldonian Theatre in Oxford. His buildings, said Fletcher, "were never over-dressed. They had a Greek elegance, rather than a Roman splendour." It was this "stripped Classicism" that the partners applied so successfully in their designs for Heal's, where the mouldings and columns are part of the structure and not merely decorative additions. "The treatment of his work was virile, simple and refined. His bent was towards the traditional form of the English Renaissance," said one obituary.

Brewer's delight in subtleties of shape found no echo in Smith's own work, such as in the deceptively simple but strong Library he designed for Armstrong College, Newcastle upon Tyne. His eye for beauty, though, led to his elegant refurbishment and extension of Brewer's spiral staircase in 1933, still standing at the back of Heal's shop.

In 1906 he was elected FRIBA and lived in St. Albans. In 1931 he took a new partner, J.A.Meikle, who ran the firm when Smith retired shortly before his death at Bournemouth in November, 1933.

FASHIONS IN DESIGN
THE ARTS AND CRAFTS MOVEMENT

Artists do not work in isolation: each is subject to influences from predecessors and teachers as well as contemporaries. Some may imitate those whom they admire and try to develop their ideas; others revolt against established traditions and become innovators.

The Industrial Revolution led to the building of towns filled with grim factories and cheap housing for the workers. Many artists and architects looked back to a Golden Age, when articles were hand-made by craftsmen and not by machines. The search for a better way of life led men like Pugin and Street to design buildings in the way they felt they had been in the Middle Ages, and mock-Gothic architecture flourished. **Augustus Pugin** (1812-52) wanted to return to a time when Christianity flourished, rather than adopt the favoured Classical principles dating from a pagan era. He was supported by **John Ruskin** (1819-1900), who thought of medieval masons as having a freedom that was not the case with the industrial workers of his day, who seemed to take no pleasure in their work.

Under Ruskin and William Morris, an attempt was made to recapture the simplicity of earlier days, when the humble cottage life seemed ideal, and when craftsmen worked in partnership to produce houses and furniture, tapestries and textiles, or jewellery and books, using their own designs.

In the 1860s, for instance, the designer Bruce Talbert created furniture, often massively made from unstained oak in strong horizontal shapes, occasionally enriched with inset panels of Gothic decoration. Others used ebony inlays, with incised gilt ornament, influenced by Japanese ideas.

Often regarded as the father of the Arts and Crafts Movement, **William Morris** (1834-96) was certainly a source of inspiration for Cecil Brewer.

Like many of the Heal family, Morris was educated at Marlborough. His father having made a successful investment in a copper mine, the family had moved from his birthplace in Wandsworth to a pleasant house near Epping Forest, where young William was free to roam amongst the trees, absorbing a love of natural foliage and amusing himself by imaginary deeds of chivalric romance.

Visits to Canterbury Cathedral as a child and to European Gothic churches as an adult encouraged in him a love of all things mediaeval. He delighted in the poems of Tennyson and the legends of King Arthur, and became acknowledged as a poet and story-teller himself.

Originally intending to enter the church, he studied architecture at Oxford and soon took up painting and furniture design, under the influence of Burne Jones and Rossetti.

His love of the life of the Middle Ages led him to despise the soul-less existence of his contemporaries working in the factories of the Industrial Revolution. The "bland tedium" of their routine production methods seemed at odds with what he saw as the joyous labour of medieval craftsmen who designed the items they made. Mass production, he felt, led to shoddy standards, and he determined to reject Victorian ostentation.

Under the influence of Ruskin, he was seized by the notion that only through applying his principles could art become again a powerful force in everyday life. He aimed to change the taste of consumers: *Have nothing in your house which you do not know to be useful or believe to be beautiful* was his famous dictum. Function was paramount. Aiming at an architectural simplicity, he opened up people's living rooms, getting rid of Victorian clutter and insisting on hand-crafted objects. This was the inspiration behind his founding of the Society for the Protection of Ancient Buildings in 1877, which tried, for instance, to overcome the use of such things as machine-made tiles in the restoration of churches.

WILLIAM MORRIS
1834 - 1896

(By permission of the Bond Agency)

Writing about what he called 'State furniture,' such as sideboards, he said, "We need not spare ornament on these, but may make them as elegant and elaborate as we can with carving, inlaying or painting; these are the blossoms of the art of furniture." [*1]

Unfortunately, though, much of Morris's career seems to have been paradoxical, infused with ironies.

When he designed stained glass windows redolent with Arthurian legends, they were in great demand for the many churches being restored by those very Gothic revivalists who were using the fussy decoration he deplored in his search for simplicity.

He wanted his artefacts to be used by ordinary people, thus enriching their drab lives; but because the former were hand made and individually designed, they were too expensive for all but the wealthiest of patrons. One German expert commented wryly on "Morris's image of an art of the people and for the people that produced such expensive things that only the upper ten thousand could consider buying them." [*2] In order to make his furniture in sufficient quantities to meet demand, therefore, he had to employ machinery.

From simple furniture with uncluttered lines, Morris moved to producing the items for which he is perhaps best known, his ornate and complex designs for wallpaper and fabrics, based on his early love of the foliage in Epping Forest. Morris wallpapers were the glory of Stanmore Hall when it was restored in the 1880s, with an elegant staircase designed by W.R.Lethaby.

The final irony in his life was that this son of a wealthy capitalist, who himself employed servants in his home, spent his last years espousing the cause of Revolutionary Socialism, trying to achieve what he saw as the necessary overturning of privilege in a society riddled with greed and inequality, and the betterment of the appalling standards of the very poor. He felt, says his biographer, "that socialism was the only way to create a healthy society in which art could flourish."

A complex pattern of influences worked on men like Norman Shaw, whose New Scotland Yard was followed by more modest house designs at Bedford Park, Chiswick, which in their turn were imitated in housing estates in Eastcote, near Pinner; or on Gerald Horsley, architect of Hatch End Station, also near Pinner; or on Edward Prior, of Harrow. Others such as Mackmurdo, Ashbee, Voysey, Lethaby, Lutyens and the landscape architect Gertrude Jekyll all had their parts to play in this development: details can be seen in histories of the Arts and Crafts Movement.

Charles Voysey (1857-1941), for instance, admired Pugin and Ruskin; he was influenced by his contemporary, A.H.Mackmurdo, but disapproved of the direction in which Norman Shaw and Lutyens were moving, with their heavier, monumental buildings in a neo-Classical style. Voysey preferred simplicity, with long ranges of mullioned windows, and simple fireplaces surrounded by glazed tiles that were bright and easy to clean.

He was one of the first as Anscombe[*3] says, "to leave behind the story book content of decoration and refine the middle class house to a basic but tasteful simplicity by taking control of every element of an interior. Like Pugin he thought that decoration should have meaning." He believed that decorative elements should be symbolic, as in his use of the stylised heart that he favoured, as did Brewer.

Externally, Voysey wanted a welcoming look, achieved by wide porches and doors. His overhanging eaves with wrought-iron brackets possibly inspired Brewer's designs for The Fives Court.

Hatch End Station, by Gerald Horsley (1862-1917).

[*1] *Anscombe page 29*
[*2] *Anscombe page 62*
[*3] *Anscombe page 104*

Spade House, Sandgate, Kent, the home of H.G. Wells.

Harrow Heritage Trust plaque on The Cocoa Tree.

A chair designed by Charles Voysey, showing the heart motif.
(By permission of the Geffrye Museum.)

Later, in 1900, just when Brewer was working on his Pinner designs, Voysey built Spade House at Sandgate in Kent for H.G. Wells. This seems very close in spirit to The Fives Court, with its tall chimneys, white-painted walls and windows under the eaves of the kind that make the Pinner house so distinctive.

His basic principle was to create austere, restrained houses in which "Repose, Cheerfulness, Simplicity and Quietness" prevailed. He designed wallpaper and furniture and even the Sanderson's wallpaper factory at Chiswick. It is said that he may have suggested the HMV trademark of Nipper, the small dog listening to His Master's Voice.

Alongside these ideals went a growing desire to improve the lot of the working man, to wean him away from drink and gambling, to enable him to live in a community of happy labourers enjoying working with wood or metal. It is perhaps no coincidence that the Cocoa Tree Tavern at the top of Pinner High Street was built as a temperance hostelry in 1878 by Ernest George and Harold Peto, two of the disciples of what came to be called the Arts and Crafts Movement, and in whose offices was trained the great Sir Edwin Lutyens.

The title was coined in 1887 by a book-designer, T.J. Cobden-Sanderson, but the pattern of development can be seen to start with Burne-Jones, Rossetti and Morris, and his Society for the Protection of Ancient Buildings— protection, that is, against some of the more iconoclastic and grandiose ideas of men like William Butterfield, who designed All Saints, Harrow Weald, or Gilbert Scott, the designer of the Vaughan Library and Chapel at Harrow School and the restorer of St. Mary's Church, Harrow.

They inspired **Philip Webb** (1831-1915), whose Red House in Bexleyheath in Kent for William Morris in 1859 was probably the first to be built in Arts and Crafts style. He used local materials and local building methods, avoiding excessive ornament. The house he designed in 1894 at Standen, near East Grinstead, is interesting for its display of Morris textiles and furniture by Ashbee and others, and for its lovely garden that seems to call to our minds the sloping site of Nower Hill House, where fritillaries flourished in the orchard. Like Nower Hill, too, it was an enlargement of an original farmhouse.

In 1881, A.H. Mackmurdo, with like-minded artists and designers, formed "The Fifteen" who met in a member's house to discuss ideas. They became the Century Guild a year later.

In 1883 came the St. George's Art Society, formed by Norman Shaw's pupils, men such as Prior, Horsley and Lethaby, meeting near St. George's Church, Bloomsbury. In the following year Prior suggested that they should form themselves into the Art Workers' Guild, ("unpractical cranks" they rather self-consciously described themselves). In 1887, under Walter Crane, they started the Arts and Crafts Exhibition Society, putting on regular exhibitions of their work. They saw as their ideal the simple natural life of the cottage-dweller, far removed from industrial wealth and ostentation.

Charles Robert Ashbee (1863-1942), famous for his metalwork, had started his School of Handicraft in the East End in 1886, to encourage workmen to take a pride in their work and to have a share in designing what they were to make, following the lines of a mediaeval guild. They made furniture, jewellery and other items that they hoped ordinary people would buy to enrich their drab lives.

It became the Guild of Handicraft in 1888, but Ashbee eventually moved out to the Cotswolds in search of rural peace and simplicity, perhaps like William Morris forgetful of the need for machinery to reduce the costs of production and so enable them to sell goods at prices that ordinary people could afford. In moving away from his industrial roots in the City, Ashbee also lost sight of his original purpose, to provide a better environment for workers in the town.

The Bromsgrove Guild of Applied Art started in 1898 under Walter Gilbert and some of their work can be seen in a memorial gate on Harrow School football fields. An early disciple was G.P.Bankart, a specialist in plaster work. *(See page 5)*

It was in the atmosphere of emphasis on the simplicity of cottage life that the Movement grew. Its followers bore in mind the paramount dictum of William Morris that designs should reflect their fitness for their purpose, with no extraneous decoration. Houses were to be designed as a whole, with the architect as artist-craftsman, responsible for fittings and furniture, gardens and paths as well as the mere shell of the building. Individual architects would employ their colleagues on details such as ceilings or furniture. "Good design," says Isabelle Anscombe, "should benefit those who made an object and those who used it." Pugin, earlier in the century, had designed not only the fittings for the Houses of Parliament, but also the door furniture, fire-places, stained glass, tiles, curtain materials, ink pots and even the jewellery used by the owners of his houses.

The homes they built were specifically designed to meet the total needs of the families that were to live in them, with children's quarters removed from the main living area, for instance.

Gardens were regarded as extra rooms, and loggias became popular as a way of helping to draw one outside. The overall tone was that of a humble, rural cottage in the Cotswolds, with low frontages, plain wooden floors, warm hearths and tall chimneys, unvarnished wood showing the natural grain, and without what one writer called the "crawling slime of ornament."

In the early years of the last century and even during the First World War, much attention was paid to German craftsmen, who were producing advanced work of a very high quality much admired by Ambrose Heal and his colleagues. Influences worked both ways, though: at an exhibition in Vienna in 1900, British designers like Ashbee and Charles Rennie Mackintosh were prominent.

You have only to walk into Pinner Parish Church by the South Porch to see, on your left, an elegant example of the Arts and Crafts style, in the memorial window to Mrs Nugent of Pinner Hall by the local Pinner artist, Louis Davis of Paines Lane. He also designed most of the windows in St. Anselm's, Hatch End.

Another contemporary artist, Clement Skilbeck, designed the window to the east of the south door in Pinner Church in memory of Edward Hogg. Skilbeck was a friend of William Morris and Edward Burne-Jones. His brother George lived at Clonard, Oxhey Lane and was the first churchwarden of St. Anselm's.

The Movement flourished for perhaps twenty or thirty years at the most until fashions changed again and then it ran out of steam, "going down a rather romantic cul-de-sac" as Julia Goodden says. Some designers, like Charles Voysey, concentrated on simplicity as can be seen in a house by him at Knotty Green, Beaconsfield. Others like Horsley employed more decoration. Generally, the Movement's plainness was replaced by the more ornate flourishes of the continental Art Nouveau and then by Art Deco. Some of its luminaries changed, too: Lutyens, for instance, like Smith and Brewer themselves, adopted a more formal, classical style far removed from the Cotswold cottage ideals of the founders, concentrating more on public buildings—shop fronts, museums and art galleries.

Now newly re-roofed, The Fives Court in Moss Lane, Pinner remains to show us a rare example of their work from a time when they were at the forefront of a revolutionary movement in domestic architecture.

DESIGN AND INDUSTRIES ASSOCIATION

In 1915, Lethaby, Heal and Brewer founded the Design and Industries Association. It was meant to encourage better design in Industry, emphasising simplicity and quality, and eliminating machine goods that were shoddy and imitative.

The DIA was based loosely on the German Werkbund, a union of artists and craftsmen who tried to ensure that manufactured goods were well designed, that teapots poured properly, for instance, and that beauty arose from an object's suitability for its purpose. Unlike the original members of the Arts and Crafts Movement, they could see a place for machinery in the economical production of goods. As the pamphlet setting out their Aims stated, probably in Brewer's own words:

"Our Association accepts the modern application of machinery in manufacture and seeks to extend the influence of Design so that all production, even of articles for commonest use, may be made with the consideration of fitness and economy which renders Workmanship beautiful. Simple things made for use are rarely ugly, such as a garden fork, a chisel, or a farmer's cart and nor are things rigidly fined down to essentials such as battleships, artillery shells, sporting guns or cricket bats. There is in fact no such thing as an ugly efficient weapon or tool, which is significant."

(Perhaps showing their wise tolerance, the DIA also published an article in 1918 from the poet Thomas Sturge Moore, who pointed out that there was no particular fitness for purpose in the wild beauty of a luxuriant rose bush and that technical excellence in a designer could not compensate for lack of divine inspiration.)

They turned their attention to everything from biscuit tins to railway stations. Frank Pick's work for London Underground, with its new stations, simple lettering and stylised map, arose directly from the Association. Cecil Brewer, who was a joint secretary and helped produce their regular journal, over-worked himself in his efforts to make the Association acceptable.

A fire grate designed by Smith and Brewer, in the Mary Ward Settlement (now the National Institute for Social Work).

In a stab at the early Arts and Crafts Society ideals (inspired by William Morris, Ashbee and others) of happy guilds of craftsmen singing as they toiled at the lathe, the DIA wrote, "The way out for the machine tender is probably rather by way of greater leisure made possible by the machine and fruitful by education, than by any attempt at joy in work corresponding to the joy of the handicraftsman (if that, indeed, be not exaggerated when the average is considered.)" (*The Beginnings of the DIA* leaflet.)

The executive committee included Ambrose Heal as Treasurer, and as Secretaries, Cecil Brewer and Hamilton Temple-Smith. The latter, being a Director of Heal's, ensured that the firm became a showcase for the Association's ideals. Other members were Frank Pick of London Underground, Marshall of Marshall & Snelgrove; Hornby of W H Smith; and Sir Kenneth Anderson, Chairman of the Orient Line.

Section of the frieze of a room at The Fives Court, showing a Celtic knot motif.

Also deeply involved was Harry Peach, of Dryad Handicrafts in Leicester, who supplied comfortable cane chairs modelled on German designs. His firm blended art school ideas, workshop skills and business acumen. Peach did much in other spheres like folk dancing to preserve the traditions and nobler qualities of an earlier age. He also founded the Council for the Preservation of Rural England. Other conservation bodies such as the National Trust and the National Footpaths Preservation Society were founded by members of the Arts and Crafts Movement.

They had great support from **William Richard Lethaby** (1857-1931), a former assistant of Norman Shaw, who had founded the Central School of Arts and Crafts in Holborn 1896, and become its first Principal. In 1914, Brewer wrote: "We had Lethaby for three hours last night for a fine discussion round the table. I wish we could hold it in public. There is opposition to our Movement - the Art Workers' Guild have refused to allot an evening to the subject even though they knew that Lethaby, their own Past Master, was to speak! Lethaby is just like a prophet on the subject and if he gets wound up should make them at least realise that there is something in it all."

But gradually, Lethaby's enthusiasm deserted him and from Brewer's letters we can see him becoming a burden rather than a help: "Lethaby is of the greatest help and encouragement." "Lethaby is to write an introduction for our pamphlet and set out the reasons for founding the Association." "Lethaby's article arrived but is not first class and is too long." "Lethaby and Burridge on educational reform are both so wrong; Lethaby is the only man who could deal with the problem but he has no fight left in him."

When seeking encouragement, Peach suggested contacting George Lansbury, Ramsay Macdonald, Charles Ashbee, H.G.Wells and Bernard Shaw. (The aim seems to have been to include as many left wing supporters as possible.) Brewer rejected Ramsay Macdonald because of "his anti-war pronouncements".

Later Chairmen included Sir Lawrence Weaver 1926-28 *(See page 2)* and Clough Williams Ellis, the builder of Port Meirion.

Clearly many of the Arts and Crafts Movement's supporters were politically minded, seeking a return to a nobler golden age away from oppressive factory employers. They spread their attention to encouraging all kinds of activities like folk songs and country crafts. In excess, their zeal could lend itself to caricatures of earnest bearded sandal-wearing types dancing round a maypole whilst dressed in home-spun and home-dyed costumes.

Martin Battersby quotes a member who claimed that they were not "dreamers in Jaeger sweaters with blue eyes fixed on supramundane peaks" but that they had "a larger vision which (perceived) that the disease of modern design in industry (was) due not to machinery but to an imperfect comprehension of its limitations and possibilities."

Among the declared aims of the DIA were:

"**Every worker owes a duty to his craft to improve the quality of his own workmanship.**"

"**Among the first necessities of Design are fitness for use and economy of production.**"

They also quoted Lethaby's dictum that

"**Art is the well-doing of what needs doing, or doing a job in a straightforward manner.**"

In 1918, just before he died, Brewer reproduced in the DIA Journal an address given back in 1863 by Mr Gladstone, in which he had praised the Wedgwood pottery factory for obeying "the law of Industrial Art, to give to every object the greatest possible degree of fitness for its purpose, making it the vehicle of the highest degree of beauty which it can bear."

Drawing of Hope by Louis Davis for a memorial window in Pinner Parish Church.

LATER RESIDENTS OF THE FIVES COURT

In the past hundred years, only four families have owned the house, though when Ambrose Heal left in 1917, it was leased to William Henry Nicholls and his wife, Mary Charlotte. In the following year, a merchant, Arthur Burleigh Nicholls and his wife Nell Duncan are recorded as having had a daughter there.

In April 1920 Dr. John Duncan Thomson bought the house. He was an expert in tropical diseases, and in 1922 visited Rhodesia to study malaria. He later became Professor of Proto-zoology at the London School of Tropical Medicine. It was the Thomsons who built a garage in 1920 and installed the chauffeur on the top storey of the house.

When Professor Thomson died, he was followed by his son, Dr. Gordon Duncan Thomson, formerly of Lodore, Cecil Park. He was a radiologist, practising in Wimpole Street, in Hounslow and latterly in the Northwood, Pinner and District Hospital. His son, John Gordon Thomson, went to Harrow School in 1946, where he was Captain of Fives and helped his boarding house to win the Fives Cup. He is now a farmer in Sussex.

In 1954 an accountant, Malcolm Moss, his wife Mary and their family became the next owners. His father was an architect and keen photographer, and a room upstairs was transformed into a dark room for him. They sold off half the large garden and Amberley Close was built on the site.

Martin and Joanne Verden moved to this Grade II Listed building in October 1982 from their home in Waxwell Lane. Like the Heals, they too have given much to the community, both having been in their time in the chair of the Pinner Association, of which Martin is now a Life Vice President. He is President of the International Steel Trade Association, but when not scouring the world for buyers of steel, he is Chairman of the Harrow Heritage Trust, Chairman of the West House Appeal and a former Chairman and now President of the Pinner Local History Society.

Joanne, as well as being passionately concerned with footpaths and the preservation of trees, has produced the book, *Ten Walks around Pinner*. She is also doing her utmost to save West House in Pinner, and was instrumental in the installation of the Peace Garden in West House grounds and in improvements to the gardens at the foot of the High Street. She is an advanced teacher of the Royal Academy of Dance. Martin and Joanne have a daughter and two sons.

Martin and Joanne Verden, the present owners.

STAFF

Over the past century, many people have helped to transform the house and garden. The excellent accommodation for staff provided by Brewer shows perhaps that William Morris's socialist ideals were still making themselves felt.

We do not know the identity of many of these workers, but a gardener named Walter Hyde, during the first world war lived in The Chase, as the Nower Hill gardener, James Milton, had done earlier. Tom Last and his wife Mary acted as chauffeur, gardener and maidservant for the Thomsons, along with an aged gardener named Chapman. Later gardeners were Ron Gunn, who died only recently and whose widow contributed to the Peace Garden in his memory, and the present custodian, David Bolton.

APPENDIX I

FAMILY TREES OF THE HEAL AND BREWER FAMILIES

HEAL

AMBROSE HEAL (1748-1812) = RACHEL HARRIS (1751-1827)

JOHN HARRIS HEAL (1772-1833) = FANNY BREWER (1782-1859)   AMBROSE HEAL (1779-1837) = MARTHA STANDERWICK (1783-1849)

JOHN HARRIS HEAL Junr (1811-1876) = ANN STANDERWICK HEAL (1810-1890)

AMBROSE HEAL Senr (of Nower Hill) (1847-1913) = EMILY MARIA STEPHENSON (1849-1938)   ANN HEAL (1835-1902) = ALFRED BREWER (1825-1901) (See below)

(Sir) AMBROSE HEAL Junr (of The Fives Court) (1872-1959) = (1) ALICE ROSE RIPPINGILLE (1860-1901)

= (2) EDITH FLORENCE DIGBY TODHUNTER (1880-1946)

CECIL AMBROSE HEAL (1896-1915)

BARBARA ALISON HEAL (1905-1906)

ANTHONY STANDERWICK HEAL (1907-1995) = THEODORA CALDWELL (1906-1992)

AMBROSE HEAL (1942-)   OLIVER HEAL (1949-)

PAMELA MARGERY HEAL (1908-83)

JOHN CHRISTOPHER HEAL (1911-85)

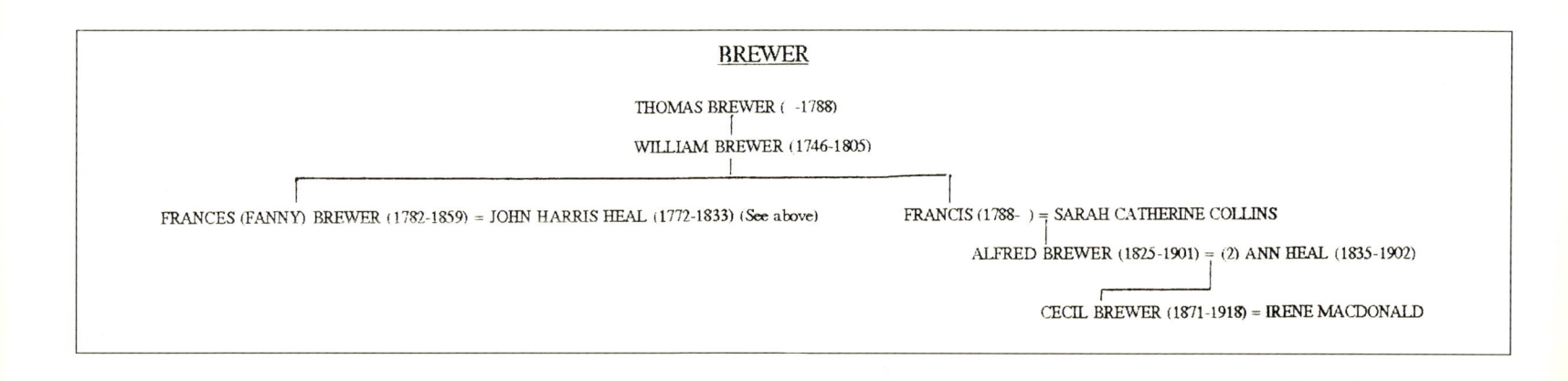

BREWER

THOMAS BREWER (-1788)

WILLIAM BREWER (1746-1805)

FRANCES (FANNY) BREWER (1782-1859) = JOHN HARRIS HEAL (1772-1833) (See above)   FRANCIS (1788-) = SARAH CATHERINE COLLINS

ALFRED BREWER (1825-1901) = (2) ANN HEAL (1835-1902)

CECIL BREWER (1871-1918) = IRENE MACDONALD

APPENDIX II

Information in appendices is largely from Goodden,
At the Sign of the Fourposter

<u>Sir Ambrose Heal's Life with Heal & Son</u>

1893	Joined family firm 27 February.
1896	Upholsterer; exhibited at Arts and Crafts Society. At about this time, Ashbee decided to move his Guild of Handicrafts from the old house in the Mile End Road, where he had founded it, to Chipping Campden. His foreman, Adams, a fine craftsman, and a few of the cabinet-makers were unwilling to uproot themselves from London, and joined Heal's staff. William Morris died.
1898	Partner in Heal's; published catalogue, *Plain Oak Furniture*.
1899	Published *Simple Bedroom Furniture*. Exhibited at Arts and Crafts Exhibition Society.
1900	Took over in charge of Heal's advertising: design of black & white chequer border gave Heal's instant identity. The Fives Court being designed.
1901	Shortly after moving to The Fives Court, he lost his wife Alice Rose.
1902	Travelled in Italy and Morocco.
1903	Holiday in Brittany with Dr Todhunter, his sister Edith and the novelist Berta Ruck (1878-1978).
1904	Married Edith Todhunter at Broad Street Registry Office, Holborn. Designed "Four-poster" trademark for Heal's.
1906	Joined Arts & Crafts Exhibition Society.
1907	Managing Director of Heal's.
1910	Elected to Art Workers' Guild (to 1959).
1912	Cecil Brewer's older brother, Maurice, made a Director of Heal's. Ambrose travelled to Austria. Heal's sales quadrupled since 1894.
1913	On death of father, elected Chairman of Heal's until January 1953; original farmhouse, Capper's Farm, later a hostel, demolished for new bedding factory. Brewer working on design for shop.
1914	To exhibition of *Werkbund* in Cologne, Germany.
1915	Helped found Design and Industries Association with Cecil Brewer; appointed Treasurer; exhibition of German and Austrian design organised by Board of Trade at Goldsmiths' Hall boosted Arts & Crafts & DIA campaign; Prudence Maufe appointed as consultant to Heal's on interior decor and exhibitions.
1916	Smith & Brewer re-built 195-6 Tottenham Court Road site.
1917	Mansard Gallery opened; Ambrose moved to Little Bekkons, Beaconsfield.
1918	Cecil Brewer died in August.
1919	Prudence Maufe became his mistress and dined with him nearly every day. Moved to Baylin's Farm, Beaconsfield. Controversial show of French paintings organised in Mansard Gallery by Sacheverell Sitwell, including Picasso & Matisse; (a Modigliani cost 30 old pence].
1920	Heal & Son, mattress makers, bedstead, bedding & down quilt manufacturers, cabinet makers, upholsterers, china & glass dealers, carpet warehousemen, & interior decorators, 193-199a Tottenham Court Rd. W1; factories and warehouses 11 Francis St & 187a Tottenham Court Rd, and 16-20 Alfred Mews, W1. (Advertisement)
1923	Visited Sweden, for Gothenburg Jubilee Exhibition; launched Orrefors Glass in England; interviewed Dodie Smith for job in February, & in 'pin neat hand' offered her job of selling woodcuts & prints in Little Gallery. Worked with Gordon Russell in Cotswolds on British Industrial Art exhibition at V & A.
1924	BBC gave King George V a wireless set designed by AH.
1925	At Paris International Exhibition.
1927	Heal's awarded Royal Warrant for Beds and Bedding. Wrote article in Print Collectors' Quarterly on the Trade Cards of Engravers.
1927-33	Affair with Dodie Smith; flat in Fitzroy Square.
1928	Elected to Bibliographical Society.
1929	Published in *Notes and Queries* an article on 65 editions of Cocker's *Arithmetic*. Ambrose owned the first edition, published in 1677.
1930	Depression: bedding sales dropped to 76% of 1926 level; AH looked for redundancies; asked staff to accept 10% salary cut. At Stockholm Exhibition: saw furniture in industrial style yet in craft tradition; returned from continent for first night of Dodie's *Autumn Crocus*.
1931	Member of Advisory Council of V & A; expensive stand at Ideal Home Exhibition: spectacular but unsuccessful display of beds including Princess & Pea and with towering four-poster designed by Mrs Maufe to counteract depression.
1932	Introduced economy furniture designed by E.W.Shepherd of Greenings in Oxford; saved finances of shop; sent out 38,000 booklets to selected customers owning a telephone.
1933	Knighted for improving design standards. Mrs Maufe designed show flats with all furnishings, and ran *White and Off White* exhibition.
1934	Elected to Royal Society of Antiquaries; sold honeybuff Wedgwood. Mrs Maufe organised *Greens of the Earth* & *Country Home* exhibition. Heal organised exhibition: *Better Furniture for Better Times*.
1935	At *Art in Industry* exhibition; Heal's 125th anniversary: *The Silver Theme in Furniture and Decoration* exhibition. Bed posts covered in silver leaf and drapes in silvery satin; Heal's store enlarged by Sir Edward Maufe.
1937	Planned to retire to Bath; took flat at 3 Marlborough Buildings, searched for suitable house. Firm of Smith & Brewer sued Heal's for breach of copyright.
1938	IRA bomb planted in new windows. ("There's always something exciting going on at Heal's.")
1939	Elected to the Faculty of Royal Designers for Industry. He made Mrs Maufe a Director of Heal's.
1939-45	Heal's made bedding and parachutes for Services; bought 125 sewing machines for them; started new subsidiary with Mrs Maufe: Heal's Wholesale and Export Ltd (later Heal Fabrics); he wrote to Dodie about making Utility Furniture, wartime transport problems, the

1940 | In February he wrote to Dodie about her wedding and was confident she had done the right thing. He was late in writing as he had been opening a Danish shop, attended by the Crown Prince of Denmark, "A perfect iceberg and about the same size."

dearth of books, "foreigners swarming all over Beaconsfield", and the arrival of evacuees at Baylin's Farm ("and not very nice clean children at that"). He was doing a roaring trade in black-out materials, and was short of cigarettes (Dodie Smith sent him some from USA). Shop hit by oil bomb and incendiaries; last V2 rocket missed shop by few yards, destroying the Whitfield Tabernacle across the road.

1940 In February he wrote to Dodie about her wedding and was confident she had done the right thing. He was late in writing as he had been opening a Danish shop, attended by the Crown Prince of Denmark, "A perfect iceberg and about the same size."

1941 Heal's fined £150 + costs when Maufe's designs for new shop front said to infringe Brewer copyright.

1944 Wrote to Dodie with review of play by Esther McCracken that mentioned her; She sent him *The Sofa and the Window*; he read it lying on a sofa in a window in a hotel in Lyme Regis, having crocked his knee hopping on a bus.

1945 Heal's acquired a building firm in Bromley, George Coulter Ltd.

1946 Lady Heal died; *Britain Can Make It* exhibition at V & A.

1951 Dodie visited him at Baylin's Farm, which he shared with Anthony & Theodora (who used to work in Heal's china department).

1952 Began to take a back seat and spend time writing books; aged 80, a widower, referred to Theo's dog as "the creature". "He was no longer himself now, removed from Heal's, just as Heal's was no longer itself without him," said Dodie Smith. Heal's designer Lucienne Day won Milan Triennale gold medal and 1st prize in American Institute of Interior Designers for Calyx fabric design; sales reached £1m.

1953 Retired; 1000 visitors a day at Heal's.

1954 Awarded Albert Medal of Royal Society of Arts for services to industrial design.

1955 Heal's bought Green & Vardy, the architectural joiners who had restored the House of Commons.

1957 Heal's appointed upholsterers and suppliers of bedding to Queen Elizabeth II.

1959 Sir Ambrose died 15 November at Baylin's Farm.

APPENDIX III

Typical Furniture Designs by Sir Ambrose Heal

1895 Oakwood stand with block printed curtains, capturing rural style of William Morris and A & C Movement;

1897 Designed simple bedroom furniture, the Newlyn and St. Ives ranges in fumed oak, with steel handles & hinges, and mahogany and pewter inlays. "The state of the furniture trade in the 1890s was was about at the deadliest," he wrote, "To me it offered the easiest possible target for fresh life."

1898 Reversible garden chair in case one side wet; library table with bookshelf legs, & chaise longue with separate adjustable leg rests.

1899 Showed 'Newlyn' bedroom furniture at sixth exhibition of Arts and Crafts Society; dressing table of Fine Feathers Suite had mirror engraved "If this be Vanity, who'd be wise?" & Wardrobe had "Fine Feathers Make Fine Birds"; as a result, commissioned by Hotel Standard at Norrkoping, Sweden, to supply all their furniture.

1900 Scored a notable success by winning a silver medal at the Paris Exhibition for a bedroom suite, part of which was shown at the V & A in 1952. AH departed from usual severe simplicity; shown on stand designed by CCB; facade framed in chequer border; check ebony and pewter inlay in oak; wardrobe with curved top; oak twin beds with peasant tapestry hangings by Geoffrey Blount; dressing table with octagonal mirror; wash stand had ruby tiles enclosed in pewter binding; writing bureau; clothes chest with removable tray to lay out dress at full length; white woodwork wall panels in apple green and white printed linen; cherry carpets and curtains; purple tiles; characteristic recessed squashed heart handles and circular latches. (*Architectural Review*, June 1900)

1903 Tallboy chest in sweet chestnut, with 5 drawers; 2 cupboards with recessed handholds and wooden latches; bedside table in sweet chestnut, with latched cupboard and extending side leaves, for John Piper. (*Beauty's Awakening* 1984)

1905 Created furniture for a cottage in Letchworth designed by F.W.Troup.

1914 Showed walnut chairs inlaid with mother-of-pearl, made by William Jones at Paris Exhibition.

1916 Black and gold sideboard.

1917 Introduced painted furniture, overcoming wartime shortage of hard-woods.

1918 New finishes including weathered oak replaced unpolished wood of earlier designs; Ambrose wrote, "There is a demand for plain, straight forward, stoutly made and properly planned and thoroughly useful furniture. Simple design and plain shapes will demand good workmanship and sound materials. Furniture should be fit for its purpose and soundly made. But we mustn't expect it cheap. There must be a watchful eye for dust traps from the wardrobe cornice to the plinth on the sideboard." (*DIA Journal* April 1918)

1922 Designed oak table and chairs for Chartwell with architect Philip Tilden. Liked metal tubing furniture & sprung mattresses. (*News Chronicle* 28.4.1933)

1925 At the Paris Exhibition he disapproved of the art deco inlays and exotically curvaceous furniture; these were frowned on by the purists of the "fitness for purpose" school.

1928/9 Waring & Gillows, Shoolbreds and the Ideal Home Exhibition all showed ultra-modern furniture; AH wrote, "The changes in furniture amounted almost to a revolution. At many of the larger stands (at the Ideal Home Exhibition) hardly an antique or reproduction was to be seen. I notice how the crowd was decidedly drawn towards the modern."

1930 Started designing with steel; at the Stockholm exhibition the Swedes designed in an industrial style yet in the craft tradition. *Modern Tendencies* exhibition in Mansard Gallery showed chromium plated bed in tubular steel designed by Leonard Thoday and made by Accles & Pollock; used steel furniture by Mies van der Rohe; equipped ladies' waiting room at Paddington Station. It was about this time that AH started a "Signed Edition" series, with signed vellum labels, stressing beauty and practicality; recessed handles did not catch on clothes; key fitted on main frame and not on opening door, so did not get lost; telephone on telescopic arm.

1933 Used oval-section steel tube for bed chassis; new booklet: *Economy with a Difference at Heal's*. He designed a sideboard-cum-cocktail cabinet in Australian walnut, with chromium bands and curved ends, a dramatic leap from the boxy look of his 1930 pieces.

1934 *Better Furniture for Better Times* catalogue; sycamore and walnut bedroom furniture by Arthur Greenwood; showed at Dorland Hall exhibition of the Design and Industries Association.

1935 *Art in Industry* exhibition at RA included AH'S chromium-banded sideboard & tubular metal dining furniture; exhibition criticised as being expensive and out of touch.

1948 In *Low Cost Furniture* exhibition in New York, first prize to two Heal's designers for storage system in birch and mahogany with aluminium legs.

1951 Heal's furniture prominent at *Festival of Britain* exhibition.

2000 Examples of Heal's furniture on display at the Victoria and Albert Museum.

Ambrose Heal's early mahogany dressing table, with inlaid pewter motifs and the inscription, "If this be Vanity, who'd be Wise?"

APPENDIX IV
Comments on Heal as a furniture maker

1895 "(He was) the only man in the furniture trade of his time who had any interest in and knowledge of design, and like all pioneers he was sniped at from all corners; but he stuck to his guns. His outlook was not just a fashion, it was a deeply felt way of life with him and affected everything he did. His sincerity gained him a small but devoted clientele. He married the Arts & Crafts idea to practicality, providing good design at a reasonable price." (Gordon Russell)

1896 When AH attempted to introduce his simply-designed pieces among the florid scrolls of "Queen Anne cabinets" and "Old English tables," with elaborate bobbin-turned legs and stretchers, he was asked by the salesmen how he could expect them to sell "prison furnishings", and the workshop craftsmen rebelled.
Heal later admitted that his first venture in simplicity in design was not an instantaneous success. Yet he persisted because he was primarily interested in expressing himself as a worker in wood and only secondarily in reforming the ornate and meretricious designs about which nobody seemed to mind.
C.R.Eastlake commended the humble Windsor chair and said that, "We have at the present time no more artistic workman in his way than the country cartwright," a remark taken to heart by Ambrose Heal. (Anscombe, page 68)
"Heal's furniture ranged from the cheap to the more expensive, made of cherry, walnut, chestnut or oak, but all was characterized by simple design and crafted details such as ebonized bandings and chip-carved plain handles." (Cumming & Caplan, 98). John Gloag said that Heal's furniture was "simple and well-proportioned; stains, glittering polishes, carved and applied ornament were rejected." (*Ambrose Heal Centenary*, in Howe, 14)

1898 First catalogue: *Plain Oak Furniture*: said to display 'quirky ingenuity'. Gleeson White produced *A Note on Simplicity of Design in Furniture for Bedrooms, with special reference to some recently produced by Heal & Son.*.

1899 Trade catalogue, *Simple Bedroom Furniture*, praised by *The Builders' Journal* for its "genuine literary and artistic interest. Simplicity, good proportion, good workmanship are its prevailing characteristics."

1900: Increasing certainty of touch in design; his products became recognised by an ever larger number of people of taste as "Heal's pieces".

1916 Cecil Brewer wrote, "His black and gold sideboard is surely a finger-post to those whose business it is to make or sell furniture in quantity. (*A Lesson to Storekeepers*)

1925 "Heal furniture has long been my admiration. I have commended it to such fortunate friends as I supposed could pay well for work of distinction. But I have been careful to tell them that Heal was not a synonym for inexpensive. But in fact Heal furniture is no more costly than commoner stuff." (Sir Lawrence Weaver, later President of the DIA.)

1930 "He transformed his shop into being a pioneer of design." (Dodie Smith)

1935 Said by Herbert Read to have become "more modish and Mayfairish at the expense of logical design."

APPENDIX V

Books & Articles by Sir Ambrose Heal

London Tradesmen's Cards of the XVIII Century
    (Batsford 1925; reprinted Dover, New York)
The Trade Cards of Engravers (Print Collectors' Quarterly, July 1927)
Cocker's Arithmetick (Notes & Queries February, 1929)
The English Writing Masters & Their Copybooks 1570-1800 (CUP 1931)
Old London Bridge Tradesmen's Cards and Tokens (in *Old London Bridge* by Gordon Hone: John Lane 1931)
The Heal Family Records (1932)
The London Goldsmiths 1200-1800 (CUP 1935)
London Shop Signs (Notes & Queries 1939)
The Signboards of Old London Shops (Batsford 1947)
The London Furniture Makers from the Restoration to the Victorian era, 1660-1840 (with R.W.Symonds) (Batsford 1953)

(With acknowledgements to the British Library.)

Heal Family Coat of Arms, granted in 1931 for the use of descendants of John Harris Heal, junior (1811-76).

BIBLIOGRAPHY

JOURNALS & REFERENCE

Architect and Building News: 15.12.1933
Architects' Journal: December 1933, December 1937 & August 1989 (Adrian Forty)
Architectural Review: 1899, 1900, 1901, 1910, 1933, 1978
Beauty's Awakening: Catalogue of the Exhibition to mark the Centenary of the Art Workers' Guild at Brighton Museum, 1984
Country Life: 7.8.1909; & 1.7.1911 [Ditton Place]; 22.4.1982
East London Record: No.19 (1998)
Heal's Catalogues 1853-1934 (David & Charles 1972)
Heal & Sons' Archives (Victoria & Albert Museum)
LAMAS Journal, 1913: Ambrose Heal: The Old Farmhouse in Tottenham Court Road
Macmillan Dictionary of Art: (Grove)
News Chronicle: April 1933
RIBA Drawings Collection
RIBA Journal 1918, 1933, 1935, 1941; etc
RIBA Manuscript Library: Collection of letters of Harry Peach and Cecil Brewer
Royal Academy Exhibitors Vol VI: 1905-70
St. Pancras Journal: November 1961
Short Guide to the National Museum of Wales: 1937
The Architect: 1918
The Builder: 1918, 1933, 1941
The Heal Collection (Harrow Reference Library)
The Heal Collection (Holborn Library)
The Times: November 1959
Who's Who in Architecture: (Technical Journals 1914)

BOOKS

Adams, Steven: *The Arts and Crafts Movement* (Tiger 1992)
Anscombe, Isabelle: *Arts and Crafts Style* (Phaidon 1991)
Ball, Alan: *The Countryside Lies Sleeping* (Riverhill Press 1981)
Battersby, Martin: *The Decorative Twenties* (Studio Vista 1969)
Benton, Tim: *Up and Down at Heal's* (Architectural Review, February 1978)
Burdick, John: *William Morris: Redesigning the World* (Tiger 1997)
Carrington, Noel: *Industrial Design in Britain* (Allen & Unwin 1976)
Chambers, James & Gore, Alan: *The English House* (Thames Methuen 1965)
Clarke, Patricia A.: *Pinner: A Pictorial History* (Phillimore 1994)
Clay: *Oxford History of Architecture* (OUP)
Conran, Terence: *Directory of Design* (Conran Octopus 1985)
Coote, Stephen: *William Morris: His Life and Work* (Alan Sutton 1995)
Cumming, Elizabeth and Kaplan, Wendy: *The Arts and Crafts Movement* (Thames & Hudson 1991/1995)
Curl, J.S.: *Oxford Dictionary of Architecture* (OUP 1999)

Davey, Peter: *Arts and Crafts Architecture: The Search for an Earthly Paradise* (Architectural Press 1980)
Davies, Pamela: *The Parish Church of St. Anselm* (1998)
Davison, T.Raffles: *Modern Homes* (George Bell & Sons 1909)
Farr, Dennis: *English Art, 1870-1940* (OUP 1978)
Goodden, Susanna: *At the Sign of the Fourposter* (Heal and Son, 1984)
Gray, A.Stuart: *Edwardian Architecture: a Biographical Dictionary* (Duckworth 1985)
Green, Sir John Little: *English Country Cottages, their Condition, Cost and Requirements* (Rural World Publishing Co. 1899)
Green, Sir John Little: *Village Industries: A National Obligation* (Rural World Publishing Co. 1915)
Grove, Valerie: *Dear Dodie* (Chatto 1996)
Heal, Ambrose: See Appendix V
Heal, Anthony S.: *A Short Biography of Sir Ambrose Heal* (Heal's 1972)
Holme, Charles (Ed.): *Modern British Domestic Architecture & Decoration* (Studio 1901)
Howe, Jacqueline: *Thesis on The Fives Court* (unpublished, 1982)
Joy, Edward Thomas: *The Charms of Country Life* (Country Life 1967)
Kaplan, Wendy (Ed.): *Charles Rennie Mackintosh* (Abbeville Press 1996)
Lethaby, William Richard: *Architecture, Mysticism and Myth* (Percival & Co. 1892)
Mansell: *Directory of British Architects 1834-1900* (1993)
Morris, William: *Hopes and Fears for Art* (Ellis and White 1882)
Muthesius, Hermann: *Das Englische Haus* (Wasmuth, Berlin 1908)
Muthesius, Hermann: *The English House*: (Transl.Seligman) (Crosby, Lockwood & Staples 1979)
Parry, Linda: *Textiles of the Arts and Crafts Movement* (Thames & Hudson 1980)
Richardson, Margaret: *Architects of the Arts and Crafts Movement* (Trefoil 1983)
Ruskin, John: *The Two Paths* (Smith, Elder & Co. 1859)
Russell, Frank: *Art Nouveau Architecture* (Academy Editions 1979)
Smith, Dorothy Gladys ("Dodie"): *Autobiographies* (4 Vols various 1967-78]
Stamp, Gavin and Goulancourt, Andre: *The English House, 1860-1914: The Flowering of English Domestic Architecture* (Faber & Faber 1986)
Watt, Quintin: *The Bromsgrove Guild* (Bromsgrove Society, 1999)
Weaver, Lawrence: *Small Country Houses* (Country Life 1911)
Woodford, F.P.: *Streets of Bloomsbury & Fitzrovia* (Camden History Society 1997)

Acknowledgements

I am immensely grateful to many people who have helped with this book. They include the writers of all the books in the Bibliography, and:

Joanne and Martin Verden, who let me into their house, and allowed me to share in its secrets. They have inspired this publication and have taken a keen and active interest in it, lending many illustrations and making the whole thing possible; Mrs Jacqueline Howe, who pioneered much of this research for her thesis in 1982; Ambrose Heal and Malcolm Barber, for allowing me into Baylin's Farm; Oliver Heal, for many helpful suggestions about the family and for his kind Foreword; Margaret Richardson of the Soane Museum for her interest in the book and her Preface; Brian Blackwood, FRIBA, compiler of the catalogue of the RIBA collection of drawings by Cecil Brewer; Mrs Mary Moss and John Gordon Thomson (both of whom recalled with affection their residence in the house); and Mr & Mrs Collins, for showing us round Nower Hill Cottage;

Charmian Baker, Patricia Clarke, Graham Elcombe, Maurice Garnham, Ken Kirkman and Tony Venis, of Pinner Local History Society; Ken Gay, of Hornsey Local History Society; Miles Green, of Beaconsfield History Society; Mr.C.Pilgrim, of Heal's; J.E.Mills, of the architects, Brewer, Smith and Brewer, who claimed no connection; R.C.Bland, Archivist, Clifton College; Peter Saunders for his photos of the house; Martin Barnes, Elliot Gay and the printers; Geraldine Beare, for the Index; J.D.C.Vargas of Harrow School, for help with fives; Valerie Grove, biographer of Dodie Smith; Miss Chesser, of Saucy Cottage, Knotty Green; and the owners of several Arts and Crafts houses in Hertfordshire, Buckinghamshire and Surrey, especially Mr Andrews of Westcott, who allowed us, though complete strangers, to see over the interior; Ptolemy Dean, FRIBA, for enthusing knowledgeably about The Fives Court and for the use of his painting of the house; and my wife for enjoying our working days out at Standen, Rodmarton, Knotty Green, Coleshill, Radnage, Westcott and several museums.

And the staff of the following:

Aylesbury Record Office; British Library; Camden History Society; Clifton College; Design and Industries Association; Family Records Centre; Geffrye Museum; Hendon Library Local Studies Centre; Holborn Library, Camden Local History Collection (for the Ambrose Heal bequest); London Metropolitan Archives; London Borough of Harrow, Reference Library (Mr Bob Thompson) (for the Heal Collection and information files); Miss Wilson of the London Borough of Harrow Building Control; The National Museum of Wales (whose Curator sent me copies of their pre-war Guide Book); The National Institute for Social Work and their Librarian; News International Syndication, for Times Newspapers; The Principal Registry of the Family Division at First Avenue House; Public Record Office; Royal Institute of British Architects' Architectural Library and Drawings Collection (Jane Collings); Society of Genealogists; Victoria and Albert Museum; V & A Archive of Art and Design (Heal & Son Ltd collection).

Picture Credits

The author's thanks for the use of illustrations are due to RIBA Architectural Library; M & J Verden; Harrow Reference Library; Ptolemy Dean; the Architectural Review; Faber & Faber; Heal's; Peter Saunders; Country Life Picture Library; Conran Octopus; Studio Vista; Geffrye Museum; Batsford; Bond Agency; J.Goodden; Harrow Observer and Joan Golland.

Every effort has been made to establish copyright holders, and I apologise for any omissions from this list.

Index:

(Numbers in italics indicate illustrations.)

Addison, Viscount 28
Albemarle Club, Piccadilly (London) 25
Albright Art Gallery (Buffalo, New York) 25
All Saints Church (Harrow Weald) 35
Allingham, Helen 11
Amadée Villa (Crouch End, London) 10
Amersham (Buckinghamshire) 24
Anderson, Sir Kenneth 37
Anscombe, Isabelle 25n, 34n, 36
The Architect and Building News 28
The Architects' Journal 22n
Architectural Association 21, 32
Armstrong College Library (Newcastle upon Tyne) 32
Arnold, Thomas 21
Art Nouveau 36
Art Workers' Guild 25, 30, 36, 38
Arts and Crafts Movement 2, 22, 24, 30, 33-6, 38
Arts and Crafts Society Exhibition 36
Ashbee, Charles Robert (1863-1942) 34, 36, 38

Baggallay, Frank 21, 32,
Bankart, G.P. 5n, 36
Battersby, Martin 38
Bayes, Gilbert 27n
Baylin's Farm (Beaconsfield, Bucks) 18, 19, 23, rain water head 19; sundial 31
Beaconsfield (Buckinghamshire) 16, 18, 19, 23, 36
Beauty's Awakening 42
Bedford, 11th Duke of 21
Bedford Park, (Chiswick, London) 34
Beesley, Alec 15
Belgium 19
Benson, W.A.S. 5n
Betjeman, Sir John 1
Bexley Heath (Kent) 35
Birmingham 12
Blount, Geoffrey 42
Bodley, G.F. 25

Boer War 11
Bolton, David 39
Bonnet Over the Windmill (D. Smith) 15
Bournemouth 32
Brewer, Alfred (1825-1901) 10, 21
Brewer, Ann (*née* Heal) 21
Brewer, Cecil Claude (1871-1918) 2, 3, 12, 16, 36, 38, 43 accident at football 12; accident at Heal's 29; *A Lesson to Storekeepers* 30, 43; as architect of The Fives Court 1, 12; awarded Godwin bursary to visit USA and Canada 25; awarded Pugin prize 21; comments on colleagues 31;death 30; described 21, 30-1; design for Heal & Son 28; design commissions 23-5, 27-8; as designer of Passmore Edwards Settlement 21-3; designs for The Fives Court *1, 3, 20*, 23, *25, 31*, 34, 35; drawing of Nower Hill House *8*; early life 21; elected to Art Workers' Guild 25; as Fellow of RIBA 25; ill-health 29-30; influenced by Arts and Crafts Movement 2; interest in German work 21n; involvement in post-war reconstruction 28-9; letter to RIBA 27; passion for octagons 16; photo of *21*; as Secretary of DIA 37
Brewer family tree 40
Brewer, Fanny *see* Heal, Fanny
Brewer, Irene (*née* Macdonald) 30n
Brighton School of Art 32
Brittany 21
Bromsgrove Guild of Applied Art 5n, 36
Burges, William (1827-81) 32
Burne-Jones, Sir Edward Coley (1833-98) 33,35,36
Butterfield, William (1814-1900) 35

Cabbage Hall *see* Nower Hill House
Cambridge 19, 32
Canterbury Cathedral (Kent) 33
Capesthorne house (Uxbridge Road, Pinner) 24
Cardiff, buildings in 27
Cathays Park, (Cardiff) 27
Central School of Arts and Crafts (Holborn) 38
Century Guild 35
Chapman (gardener) 39

Chelsey Bunn Baker, trade card *17*
Chiswick (London) 34, 35
Chorleywood (Herts) 2
Clapperton. T.S. 27n
Clifton College 12, 21
Clonard house (Oxhey Lane, Pinner) 36
Cobden-Sanderson, T.J. 35
Cocoa Tree Tavern (Pinner) 35; plaque on *35*
Coleshill (Buckinghamshire) 24
Council for Industrial Design 28
Council for the Preservation of Rural England 38
Crane, Walter 36
Crouch End (London) 10, 12
Cuckfield (Sussex) 25

Darvel, James, builder 10
Davey, Peter 2
Davis, Louis 36; drawing of Hope for memorial window *38*
Dean, Basil 15
Dean, Ptolemy, water-colour of The Fives Court *x*; architect 2
Design Council 28
Design and Industries Association (DIA) 5, 28, 30, 31, 37-8; Journal of 42
Dickens, Charles 9
Ditton Place (Cuckfield, Sussex) 25
Dorking (Surrey) 25
Dove, Daisy (*née* Heal) 19
Dryad Handicrafts 38
Dublin 19

East Grinstead (Sussex) 35
East House (Moss Lane, Pinner) 24
Eastcote (nr. Pinner) 34
Eastlake, Charles R. 43
Edwards, John Passmore 21
Ellis, Clough Williams 38
Empire Theatre (Leicester Square, London) 9
Epping Forest (Essex) 33, 34
Euston Station (London) 22

Evans, David 27n
Everyman Theatre (Hampstead, London) 15

Farr, Dennis 22
'The Fifteen' 35
Firgrove house (Nower Hill, Pinner) 12
First World War 5, 24, 28-9, 36, 39
Fitzwilliam Museum (Cambridge) 32
The Fives Court (Pinner) 1-7, 23-4, 36; being built *24*; births at 19; Brewer's designs for *1, 3, 20, 25, 31*; Celtic knot motif at *37*; children's rooms 7; conception for 2; deaths at 19; design features 23, 25; entrance to 3; extension to 3; as family home 5; first occupied by Ambrose Heal 11-12; fives court and gardens *1, 2, 7*; game of fives *2*; later residents of 39; layout of rooms 5, 7; as listed building 1; location of *iv, vi,* 1; loggia *6*; modern view of *4*; music room 5, *6*; north elevation *viii*; perambulatory 5; plasterwork in 5; realisation of 2-3; re-roofed 36; rose arches *6*; as seen from Nower Hill *24*; as seen from Tooke's Green *50*; servants' quarters 7; sketches by Raffles of *4*; staff of 39; sub-let 18, 39; west elevation of *x, 6*
Fletcher, H.M. 22, 24, 28, 32
Forbes & Tate 18
Forbes, Thomas 24
Forty, Adrian 22n
Frith Manor (Mill Hill, London) 10
Furniture Makers' Guild 19

Garbe, Richard 27n
George, Sir Ernest (1839-1922) 35
German: authorities 22, 34; craftsmen 36; designers 21n;
Gibbins, J.G. 32
Gilbert, Walter 36
Gilbert, Sir W.S. 23
The Glade (*later* Whytewayes) (Harrow Weald) 24
Gladstone, William Ewart 38
Glasgow School of Art 22

Gloag, John 43
Golders Green cemetery (London) 30
Goodden, Julia 18, 36, 41
Graham & Biddle 12
Graham family 10
The Grange house (Church Lane, Pinner) 10
Grass Farm (Finchley, London) 10
Great Exhibition (London 1851) 9
Great Western Railway (GWR) 14
Green & Vardy 42
Greenaway, Kate (1846-1901) 11
Greenwood, Arthur 43
Grimsdyke house (Harrow Weald) 23
Guild of Handicraft 36
Guildford Cathedral (Surrey) 14, 28
Gunn, Ron 39

Harris, Rachel *see* Heal, Rachel
Harrow Heritage Trust 5, 39; plaque *35*
Harrow on the Hill 23
Harrow Reference Library 11
Harrow School 36, 39; memorial gate 36; Music School 23; Speech Room 32; Vaughan Library and Chapel 35
Harrow Weald 23, 24, 35
Haslemere (Surrey) 30n
Hatch End (Middlesex) 36
Hatch End Station by Horsley 34; view of *34*
Headstone Lane Station 1
Headstone Races 11
Heal & Son 18; accident to employer 29; advertisements and posters *9, 16 18*; Brewer's design for *28*; copyright case 32; drawing office 19; expansion of 11, 28, 29; Mansard Gallery 14, 18; move to Tottenham Court Road (1840) 9; near Oxford Street 9; new store built (1854) 9; spiral staircase *31*, 32;views of *27, 29*; Wholesale & Export Ltd 41
Heal, Alice Rose (*née* Rippingille) (1860-1901) 5, 12; memorial to *13*
Heal, Ambrose (1748-1812) 9

Heal, Ambrose (1847-1913) 10-11, 23
Heal, Ambrose (1942-) 19
Heal, Sir Ambrose , Jr (1872-1959) 1-3, 11, 23, 36, 37; attitude to money 15; books and articles by 13,44; chronology of life and work at Heal & Son 41-2; death of 18; described 12, 13; early life 12; as friend of Brewer 29; as friend of Dodie Smith 14-15; furniture commented on 43-4; furniture designs by 16, 18, *18*, 42-3, *43*; as historian, antiquarian and writer 12-14; influence too great 31; interest in calligraphy and tradesmen's cards 13-14; interest in costume, heraldry and typography 13; knighted 16; marriages 12, 23; mistresses of 14, 15; photo of *12*; as sportsman 1; trade cards from book by *17*; as young man *3*
Heal, Ann Standerwick (1810-90) 10
Heal, Anthony Standerwick (1907-95) 7, 19, *19*
Heal, Barbara (1905-6) 19
Heal, Cecil Ambrose (1896-1915) 12, *14, 15,* 19
Heal Collection 11
Heal, Edith (*née* Todhunter) (1880-196) 5, 12, 18; expecting child *14*
Heal, Emily Maria (*née* Stephenson) (1849-1938) 11
Heal family: children in garden *14, 15, 19*; coat of arms *44*; dog, pony and trap *15*; in photo with Tooveys *2*; family tree 40; history of 9-18
Heal, Fanny (*née* Brewer) (1782-1859) *9*, 9
Heal, Frank (barrister) 10
Heal, Harris 10
Heal, John Christopher (1911-85) 19
Heal, John Harris (1772-1833) 9
Heal, John Harris Jr. (1811-76) *9*, 9-10,
Heal, John (leather merchant) 10
Heal, Oliver (1949-) ix, 7, 19
Heal, Pamela (1908-83) 19
Heal, Rachel (*née* Harris (1751-1827) 9
Heal, Ralph 19
Heal, Theodora (1906-92) 19
Hedingham Castle (Essex) 21
High Wycombe (Buckinghamshire) 30
HMV 35

Hogarth, William 17
Hogg, Edward 36
Hornby, C.H. St. John 37
Horsley, Gerald (1862-1917) 34, 36
Houses of Parliament 36
Howe, Jacqueline 5n
Hyde, Walter 39

I Capture the Castle (D. Smith) 15
Industrial Revolution 33
International Steel Trade Association 39

Jekyll, Gertrude 34
Jones, William 42

Kaplan, Wendy 22
King's College Hospital (London) 30n
Kingston Deverill (Gillingham, Dorset) 9
Knight, Buxton 11
Knotty Green (Beaconsfield, Bucks) 36

Lansbury, George 38
Last, Mary and Tom 39
Lecture Rooms (Mill Lane, Cambridge) 32
Lethaby, William Richard (1857-1931) 22, 24, 34, 36, 38
Letchworth (Herts) 16
Little Barley End, (Tring, Herts) 24
Little Bekkons house (Beaconsfield, Bucks) 18
Lockyer, J. Morant 9; design by *27*
Lodore house (Cecil Park, Pinner) 39
London 34; Bloomsbury 21-2, 29, 36; Chiswick 34, 35; Crouch End 10, 12; East End 21, 36; Finchley 10; Golders Green 30; Hampstead 15; Holborn 38; Leicester Square 9; Mill Hill 10; Oxford Street 9; Piccadilly 25; Tavistock Place 21-2; Tavistock Square 21; Tottenham Court Road 9, 28, 29; Wandsworth 33
London and Middlesex Archaeological Society 11
London Tradesmen's Cards of the XVIII Century (A. Heal) 13

London Underground 37
Louvre (Paris) 27, 32
Lutyens, Sir Edwin Landseer (1869-1944) 34-36

Macdonald, George 30n
Macdonald, Greville 30n
Macdonald, Irene *see* Brewer, Irene
Macdonald, (James) Ramsay 38
Mackintosh, Charles Rennie (1868-1928) 22, 36
Mackmurdo, Arthur Heygate (1851-1942). 34, 35
Macmillan Dictionary of Art 25, 28
Malvern College 19
Mansard Gallery (Heal's) 14, 18
Marlborough College 1, 12, 19, 33
Marshall & Snelgrove 37
Mary Ward Settlement 21-3; fire grate *37*; outside views of *22, 23*
Maufe, Sir Edward (1883-1974) 14, 18, 28
Maufe, Prudence (d.1976) 14
Meikle, J. A. 28, 32
Millard, Walter 32
Milton, James 39
Moore, Thomas Sturge 37
Morris, William (1834-96) 2, 30n, 33-36; sketch of *33*
Moss, Malcolm and Mary 39
Muthesius, Hermann 22

Nash, John 27
National Footpaths Preservation Society 38
National Museum of Wales (Cardiff) *26*, 27
National Trust 38
Nayland Sanatorium (Suffolk) 23
New Scotland Yard (London) 23, 24
New York 25
Newcastle upon Tyne 32
Nicholls, Arthur Burleigh and Nell Duncan 39
Nicholls, William Henry and Mary Charlotte 39
Nipper the dog (HMV mascot) 35
Northwood (Middlesex) 28
Northwood, Pinner & District Hospital 39

Nower Hill Cottage (Pinner) 24; door knocker *31*
Nower Hill House (Pinner) vi, 3, 6, 7, 10, 21, 23, 35, 39; bought by Ambrose Heal (1895) 10; Christmas card design *11*; drawn by Brewer *8*; handbill for garden party at *11*; known as Cabbage Hall 11; octagonal hall *23*; poster advertising sale of *10*; sundial from *31*
Nugent, Mrs 36

On the Encouragement of Small Industrial Centres... report (1918) 28-9
One Hundred and One Dalmatians (D. Smith) 15
'The Orchard' (Chorley Wood, Herts) 2
Orient Line 37
Oxford 32

Paines Lane Cemetery, Ambrose and Emily Heal buried 11; memorial to Alice Rose Heal *13*
Paris 27, 32; Exposition (1900) 5n
Passmore Edwards Settlement (Bloomsbury, London) 21-3
Peace Garden (West House, Pinner) 39
Peach, Harry 38
Pegram, Bertram 27n
Penn (Buckinghamshire): grave of Sir Ambrose Heal at 18; Churchyard cross by Maufe 18; death of Anthony Heal at 19
Peto, Harold Ainsworth 35
Pevsner, Sir Nikolaus 2, 22
Pick, Frank 37
Pinner (Middlesex) *ii, iv, vi*, 1, 7, 10, 11, 34; Amberley Close 6, 39; Barrow Point 11; Blackgates (Monks' Walk) 1, 23; The Chase 24, 39; Church Lane *iv, vi*, 10, 19, 23; East End 11; Headstone 2, 11; High Street *vi*, 1, 11, *15*, 35, 39; Moss Lane *iv, vi*, 1, 3, 7, 11, 12, 23, 24, 36; Nower Hill, *vi*, 1, 10, 12; Oxhey Lane 36; Paines Lane, 5, 36; Tooke's Green 7, 23, *50*; Uxbridge Road 24; Wakehams Hill 1, *2*; Waxwell Lane 11, 39
Pinner Association 5, 39

Pinner Hall 36
Pinner Horticultural Society 11
Pinner House 1
Pinner Local History Society 5, 39
Pinner Local Studies Centre 11
Pinner Men's Club 11
Pinner Parish Church 11, 36; drawing for window in 38
Pinner Park 1
Pinnercote house (Paines Lane, Pinner) 5; garden party at 7
Playfair, Sir Nigel 15
Port Meirion 38
Pretty Corner (Northwood, Middlesex) 28
Prior, Edward Schroeder (1852-1932) 23, 34, 36
Pugin, Augustus Welby Northmore (1812-52) 33, 36

Radnage village (Buckinghamshire) 28, 29, 30
RAF Memorial (Runnymede, Surrey) 28
Raffles, Thomas, sketches of reception rooms at The Fives Court 4
Read, Herbert 44
Red House (Bexley Heath, Kent) 35
RIBA Journal 22
Richardson, Margaret ix, 22
Rippingille, Alexander 12
Rippingille, Alice Rose *see* Heal, Alice Rose
Robert Elsmere (M. Ward) 21
Robinson, Fitzroy 28, 29
Robinson, William Heath 7
Rockstone House (Paines Lane, Pinner) 5
Rossetti, Dante Gabriel (1828-82) 33, 35
Rowntree, Seebohm 22
Royal Academy 11, 32
Royal Academy Schools 21, 25, 32
Royal Designer for Industry 41
Royal Institute of British Architects (RIBA) 25, 30, 32; Godwin Bursary 25, 32; letter from Brewer to 27; Pugin studentship 21
Rugby School 21

Runnymede (Surrey) 28
Rushymead house (Coleshill, Bucks) 24
Ruskin, John (1819-1900) 30n, 33
Russell, Sir (Sydney) Gordon (1892-1980) 19, 43

St. Albans (Hertfordshire) 32
St. Anselm's Church (Hatch End, Middlesex) 36
St. George's Art Society 36
St. George's Church, (Bloomsbury, London) 36
St. John's Church (Pinner) 1, 11
St. Mary's Church (Harrow, Middlesex) 35
St. Pancras Library (London) 11
St. Pancras Old Church (London) 21
St. Pancras Station (London) 22
Sanderson's wallpaper factory (Chiswick, London) 35
Sandgate (Kent) 35
School of Handicraft (East End, London) 36
Scott, Sir George Gilbert (1811-78) 35
Second World War 5, 28
Shaw, George Bernard 38
Shaw, Richard Norman (1831-1912) 22, 23, 34, 36, 38
Sheldonian Theatre (Oxford) 32
Sidney Sussex College, (Cambridge) 19
Skilbeck, Clement 36
Skilbeck, George 36
Slade School of Art 12
Smith, Arthur Dunbar (1866-1933) 2, 21, 30, 36; awarded Godwin Bursary 32; death of, 32; described 32; designs by 24; early life 32; elected FRIBA 32; influenced by Arts and Crafts Movement 2; photo *32*
Smith and Brewer 3, 5n, 10; designs by 21-8; work described 24-5; work illustrated *viii, ix, 1, 3, 4, 6, 8, 20, 22-3, 23, 24, 25, 26, 28, 29, 31, 37, 50*
Smith Dodie (C. L. Anthony) (1896-1990) 14-15, 18, 44
Soane, Sir John (1753-1837) 5
Society for the Protection of Ancient Buildings 33, 35

The Sofa and the Window (D. Smith) 42
Spade House (Sandgate, Kent) 35, *35*
Springbank house (Westcott, Surrey) 25, *25*
Stamp, Gavin viii
Standen House (East Grinstead, Sussex) 35
Stanmore Hall (Middlesex) 34
Steiner, Rudolf (1861-1925) 22
Stephenson, Emily Maria *see* Heal, Emily Maria
Stocks Farm (Tring, Hertfordshire) 24
Street, George Edmund (1824-81) 33
Sudbury (Suffolk) 23
Suffragettes 5; garden party at Pinnercote *7*; notepaper *7*

Talbert, Bruce 33
Temple-Smith, Hamilton 37
Ten Walks Around Pinner (J. Verden) 39
Tennyson, Alfred Lord (1809-92) 33
Terrero, Mrs Jane 5
Thomas, Dunbar 12n
Thomson, Dr Gordon Duncan 39
Thomson, Dr John Duncan 39
Thomson, John Gordon 39
Thurber, James 15
Tilden, Philip 42
Todhunter, Edith *see* Heal, Edith
Toovey, Arthur 19
Toovey family 2
Torquay (Devon) 12
Town End Farm (Radnage, Buckinghamshire) 30
Toynbee Hall (East End, London) 21
Tring (Hertfordshire) 24
Troup, F. W. 16, 42
Troup Winifred (*née* Macdonald) 30n
University Hall (London) 21
Uthwatt, Mr Justice 32
Uxbridge Road (Pinner, Middlesex) 24

Verden, Martin and Joanne, ix, 5, 39, *39*
Verden, Mr & Mrs Mark 5
Verden, Phyllis 5

Vienna Exhibition (1900) 36
Vintage Sports Car Club 19
Voysey, Charles Francis Annesley (1857-1941) 2, 22, 34-6; chair by *35*

W. H. Smith & Sons 37
Ward, Mrs Humphry 21, 22, 24,
Warwick (Warwickshire) 12
Weaver, Lawrence 2, 38, 43-4
Webb, Philip (1831-1915) 35
Webb, Sidney James (1859-1947) 22

Wedgwood & Sons 38
Wells, Herbert George 35, 38
Werkbund 37
West House (Pinner) 39
Westcott (Dorking, Surrey) 25; view of house at *25*
Westgate (Kent) 12
White, Gleeson 43
Whytewayes *see* The Glade
Woburn Lodge (London) 9
Women's Social and Political Union 5
Woodbridge C. A. 23

The Fives Court and Nower Hill House seen from Tooke's Green before the First World War.
(By Courtesy of Sylvia Venis)